Australian Signpost MATHS

2

Mentals

Alan McSeveny Diane McSeveny-Foster Rachel McSeveny

Introduction

Using the Mentals books

Each unit of the Mentals Book is programmed to review content from the previous two units of the Student Book. For example, Mentals Book Unit 5 can be used to review Student Book Units 3 and 4 while Student Book Unit 5 is being taught. Unit 5 from both books should be completed in the same week.

Presentation

- The content of the strands Number and Algebra, Measurement and Geometry, and Statistics and Probability is covered thoroughly.
- Essential skills are explained.
- Language, graphs, problem solving and tables are given a high profile.
- Mathematics is applied to real-life situations wherever possible.

Mixed-topic Questions

The units present questions in a mixed-topic format.

- This is essential for thorough understanding and continuous review.
- It will allow the teacher to discover weaknesses that could otherwise pass unnoticed.
- The approach reflects real life: similar questions don't often occur together.
- It provides a real test of understanding.

If You Do Not Use a Student Book

These books are invaluable to those who do not use a student book, as they ensure both thorough coverage and constant review of the syllabus content.

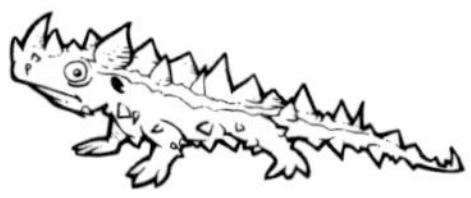

ID Cards

- The ID cards on pages 4 and 5 review the terms essential to success in this course.
- These cards can be used over and over.

You can't do the maths if you don't know the language!

Multiple-choice Questions

The multiple-choice questions on page 76 introduce a variety of question types.

- *Three headers on each double-page spread provide an opportunity for discussion. Suggestions are given on page 3.*
- *Cartoons make mathematics more appealing.*
- *There are two lizards hidden on each page for students to find.*
- *The third section of each unit usually contains counting exercises in the border.*
- *Each unit has one activity at the base of the left-hand page. Tables in addition, subtraction and multiplication (10 and 2 times) are provided.*

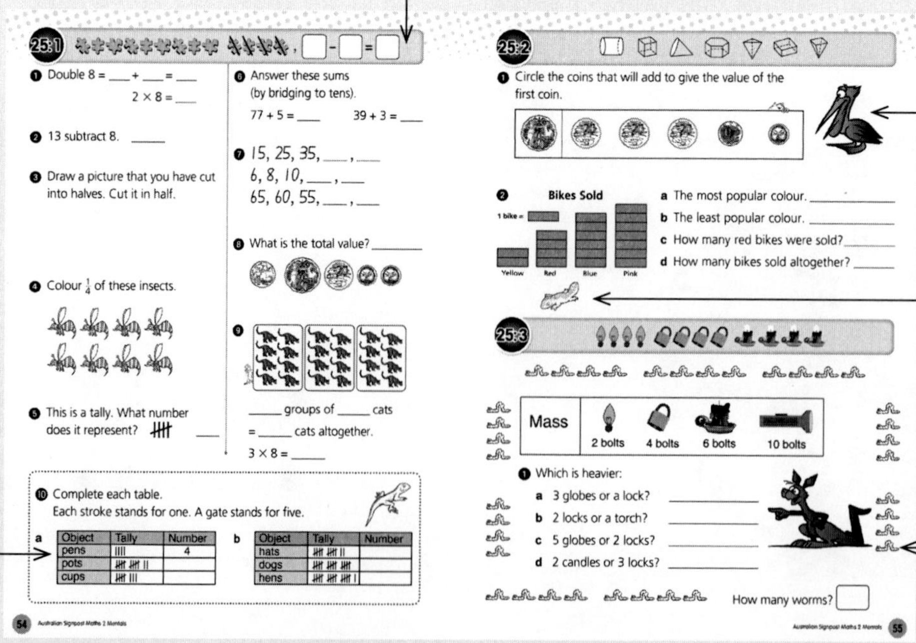

 • *AUSTRALIAN SIGNPOST MATHS 2 MENTALS* • ISBN 978 1 4886 2180 2

2 Contents

Unit Header Activities

1:1 Addition, 10 + 2 (Q5)
2:1 Cut each item in half (Q1).
3:1 Position, 3rd from the left (Q4)
4:1 Colour half of this group
5:1 Subtraction, 8 – 2 (Q1)
6:1 Subtraction, 8 – 5
7:1 Counting by 5s
8:1 Digital time, o'clock
9:1 2 groups of 4 (Q6)
10:1 Subtraction, 7 – 3 (Q5, 10)
11:1 Multiplication, 4 × 2 (Q1)
12:1 Doubles (Q6)
13:1 Addition, 6 + 7 (Q1)
14:1 Circle half of the group.
15:1 Multiplication, 3 × 4 (Q6)
16:1 Multiplication, 3 × 3
17:1 Multiplication, 3 groups of 4
18:1 Adding multiples of 10 (Q8)
19:1 Subtraction, 9 – 3 (Q2)
20:1 Estimate how many
21:1 Money: recognising coins (Q3)
22:1 Division, 3 groups of 8 (Q5)
23:1 3D shapes: edges, corners?
24:1 Multiplication, 3 × 3 (Q1, 4)
25:1 Subtraction, 13 – 4 (Q2)
26:1 Subtraction, 10 – 3
27:1 Multiplication, 3 × 3 (Q1, 6)
28:1 Multiplication, 4 × 2 (Q1)
29:1 Counting on from 127
30:1 Multiplication, 5 × 3 (Q3)
31:1 Addition, 8 + 6
32:1 Division 12 ÷ 2 (Q1)
33:1 Multiplication, 3 × 4 (Q4)
34:1 Addition, 9 + 4 (Q4)
35:1 Multiplication, 5 × 2 (Q3)

1:2 Combinations to 10 (Q1)
2:2 Subtraction from 10 (Q1)
3:2 Addition, 5 + 5 (Q2)
4:2 Time: o'clock (Q2)
5:2 Addition, 10 + 2
6:2 Weekdays
7:2 Subtraction: difference (Q2)
8:2 4 groups of 3 (Q1, 2)
9:2 Colour one quarter.
10:2 Ordinal numbers
11:2 3 groups of 3 (Q3)
12:2 Subtraction, 10 – 4
13:2 3 groups of 3
14:2 4 groups of 3
15:2 What is on the right/left?
16:2 10 shared by 5 (Q1)
17:2 3 groups of 4 (Q2)
18:2 Months of the year
19:2 Position, 5th, 12th
20:2 Multiplication, 2 × 4
21:2 2 groups of 3
22:2 Multiplication, 5 × 3
23:2 Discussion of 3D objects (Q1)
24:2 3D objects: edges, corners?
25:2 Money: value of coins
26:2 Counting by 2s, 14 lots of 2
27:2 Tallies
28:2 Multiplication, 3 × 2 (Q1)
29:2 Grouping, 2s in 12
30:2 Position: 5th, 12th (Q2)
31:2 Groups of 5, ordinals
32:2 Flip, slide, turn
33:2 Fraction shaded?
34:2 Multiplication, 4 × 2
35:2 Left, right and middle

1:3 Counting
2:3 Circle the parallel lines.
3:3 Addition, 5 + 4
4:3 Counting by 5s
5:3 Counting on, 7 + 3
6:3 Patterns on a number line
7:3 Addition, 9 + 6 + 3
8:3 Circle half of the shapes.
9:3 Halves
10:3 2D shapes
11:3 Money: notes
12:3 Addition, 3 + 3 + 7
13:3 Subtraction, 10 – 6 – 2
14:3 Trapeziums and kites
15:3 Digital time
16:3 How many groups of 2?
17:3 Number line addition
18:3 3 groups of 8
19:3 Playing card suits, 4 + 4 + 4
20:3 6 groups of 4
21:3 Addition, 5 + 5 + 5 + 5
22:3 Multiplication, 3 × 8
23:3 Pattern of 2D shapes
24:3 3D objects (face, corners, edges)
25:3 Comparing mass
26:3 Analogue time
27:3 Identifying and adding coins
28:3 Addition, 10 + 10
29:3 Identifying and adding coins
30:3 Adding amounts of money
31:3 Money: $5, $10, $20
32:3 3 + 5, 5 + 3, 8 – 3, 8 – 5
33:3 Flip, slide, slide, turn
34:3 Fractions of a whole
35:3 2D shapes

ID Card A

Do not write on this card.

1

+

a__________

2

−

s__________

3

×

m__________

4

÷

d__________

5

=

is e______ to

6

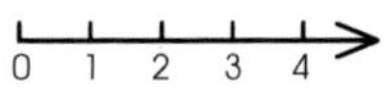

n__________

l__________

7

1st, 2nd, 3rd, 4th ...

o__________

n__________

8

o___ b______

9

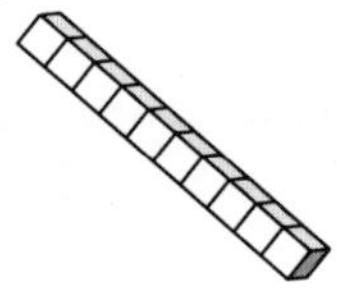

t__________

b__________

10

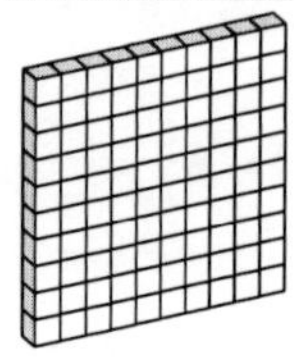

h__________

b__________

11

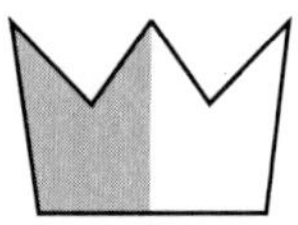

$\frac{1}{2}$

h__________

12

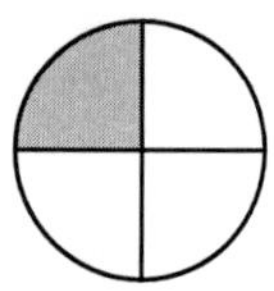

$\frac{1}{4}$

q__________

13

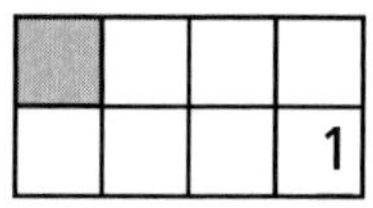

$\frac{1}{8}$

e__________

14

$

d________ sign

15

g________ coins

16

s________ coins

17

$____ notes

18

$____ notes

19

$____ notes

20

$____ notes

21

$____ notes

22

3 o'________

23

h_____ p_____ 9

24

q__________

p_______ 4

25

q__________

t_______ 8

26

3:00

d_____t______

27

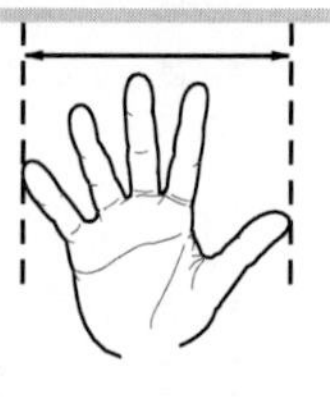

h__________

s__________

28

e______ a_______

b__________

29

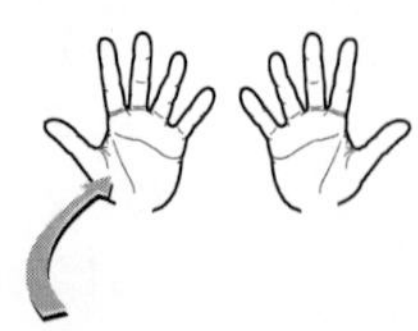

l_____ hand

30

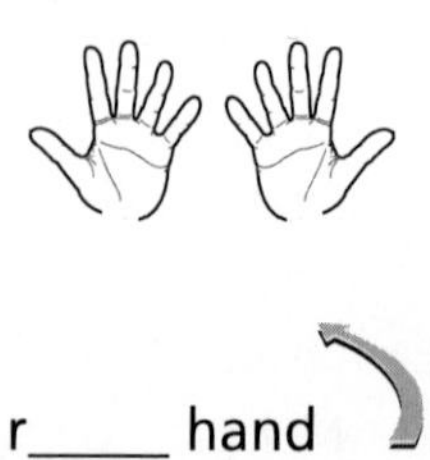

r_____ hand

ID Card B

Do not write on this card.

1
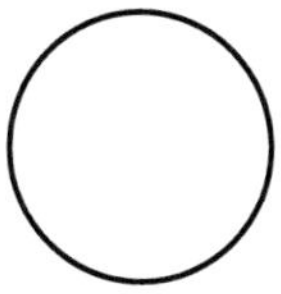
c__________

2
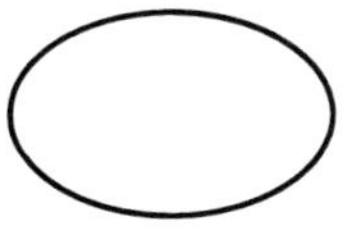
o__________

3
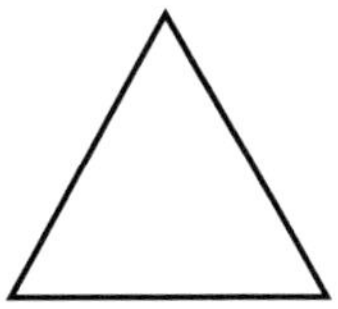
t__________

4

s__________

5
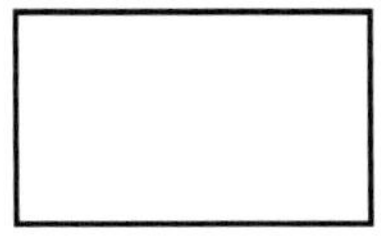
r__________

6
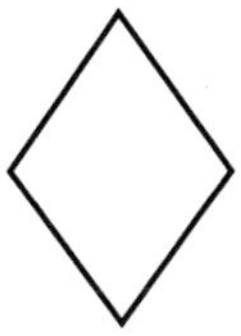
r__________

7
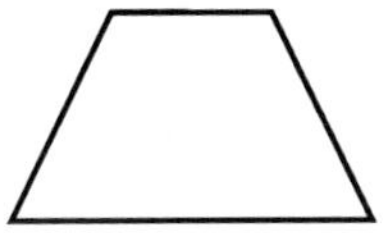
t__________

8
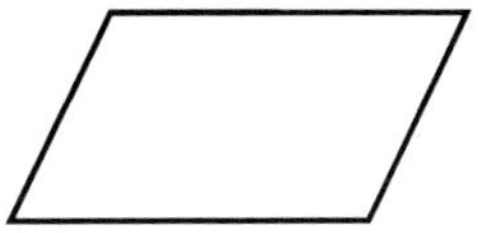
p__________

9
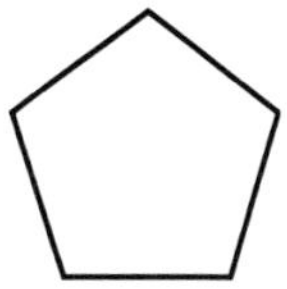
p__________

10
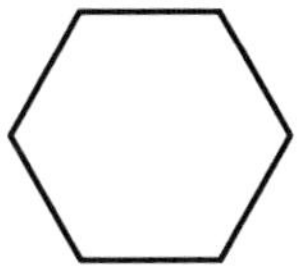
h__________

11
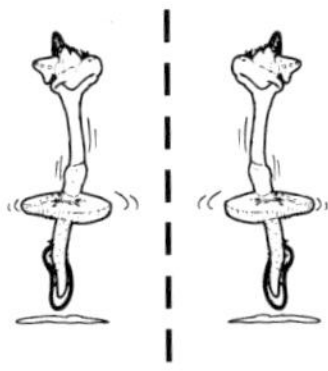
f__________

12
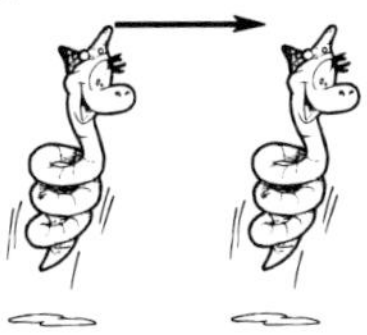
s__________

13

t__________

14
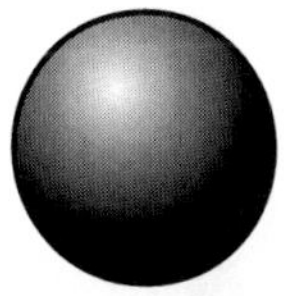
s__________

15
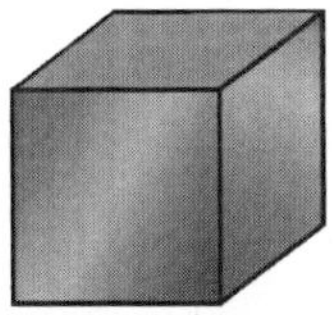
c__________

16

c__________

17
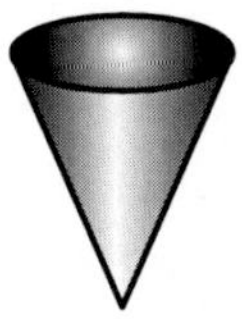
c__________

18
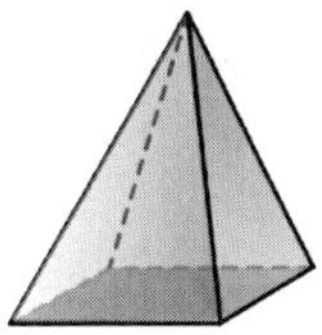
p__________

19
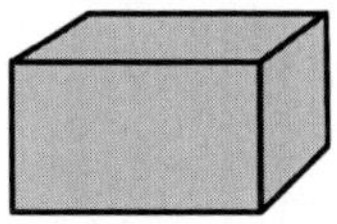
p__________

20
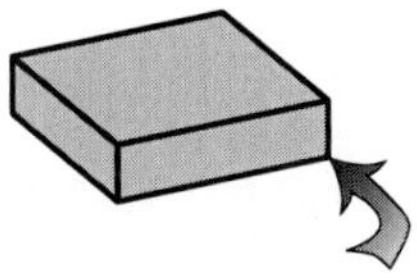
c__________

21
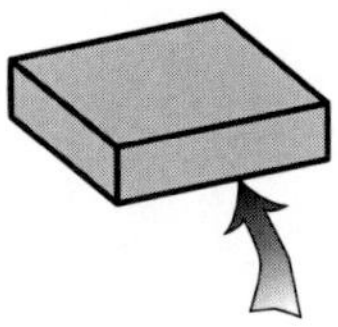
e__________

22
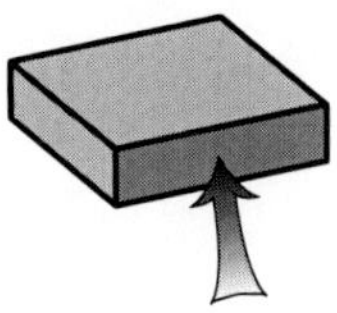
f________

23

f____ surface

24

c_____ surface

25

s______ line

26

c_____ line

27

z_____ line

28
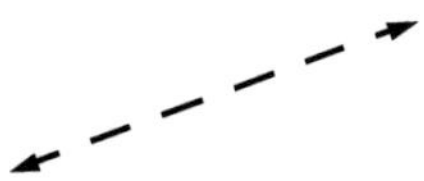
b_____ line

29

p_____ lines

30

t______

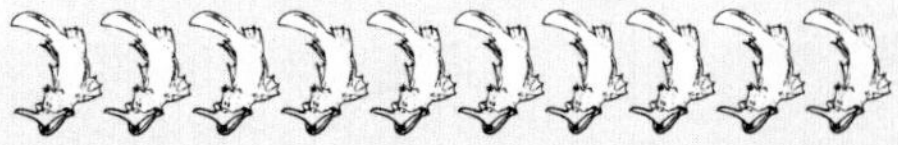 + 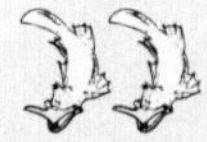 ☐ + ☐ = ☐

1 5 – 2 = ____

10 – 2 = ____

2 a △, ○, △, ○, ____, ____

b □, ▭, □, ▭, □, ____, ____

3 The time is

____ o'clock.

4 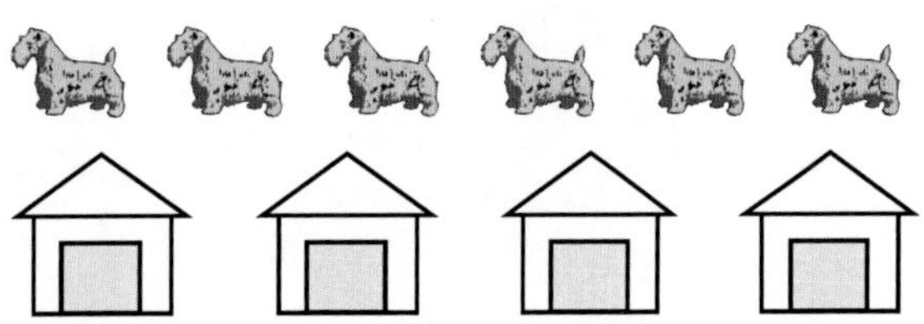

How many more dogs than kennels? ____

5 13 plus 4 equals ____.

5 Write the name of each numeral.

2 ____________________

4 ____________________

7 ____________________

11 ____________________

20 ____________________

7 Draw lines to match.

5c | 10c | 20c | 50c

8 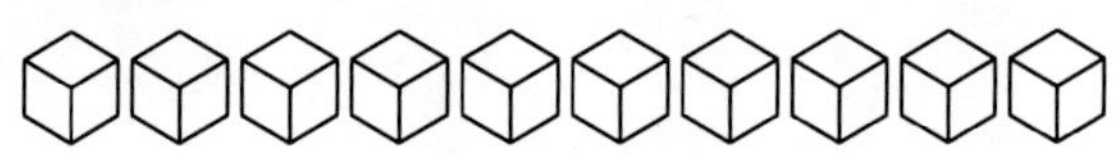

- Colour the **1st** block.
- Tick the **4th** block.
- Cross out the **9th** block.
- Circle the **6th** block.

9 Fill in the grid.

21	22	23		25	26		28		30
31	32				36	37	38		
41		43		45		47		49	

 ISBN 978 1 4886 2180 2

1:2

☐ suns

❶ Use the suns above to answer these questions.

a 2 + 6 = ____ b 4 + 3 = ____ c 4 + 4 = ____

d 3 + 7 = ____ e 8 + 2 = ____ f 3 + 3 = ____

❷ Write the time in words and numerals.

a

____

[:]

b

____

[:]

c

____

[:]

Half past nine

9 : 30

Half

❸ Write the number.

1 more than: 36, ____ 49, ____ 63, ____ 72, ____ 95, ____

1:3

☐ balls

❶ Fill in the missing numerals.

a 61, 62, ____, ____, ____, ____, 67, ____, ____

b 87, 88, ____, ____, ____, ____, 93, ____, ____

c 48, 49, ____, ____, ____, ____, 54, ____, ____

d 30, 29, ____, ____, ____, ____, 24, ____, ____

 • *AUSTRALIAN SIGNPOST MATHS 2 MENTALS* • ISBN 978 1 4886 2180 2

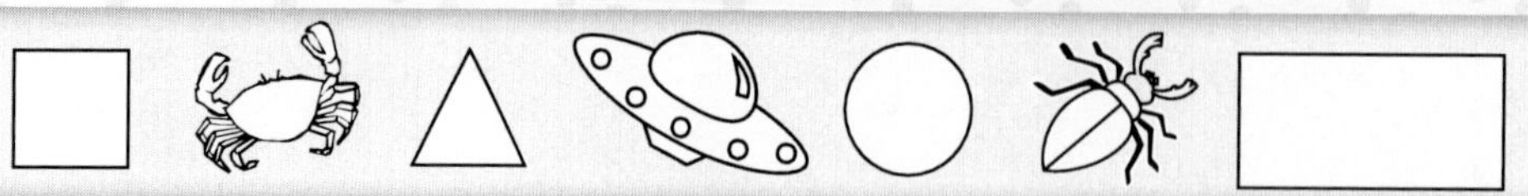

❶ Match the shapes and names.

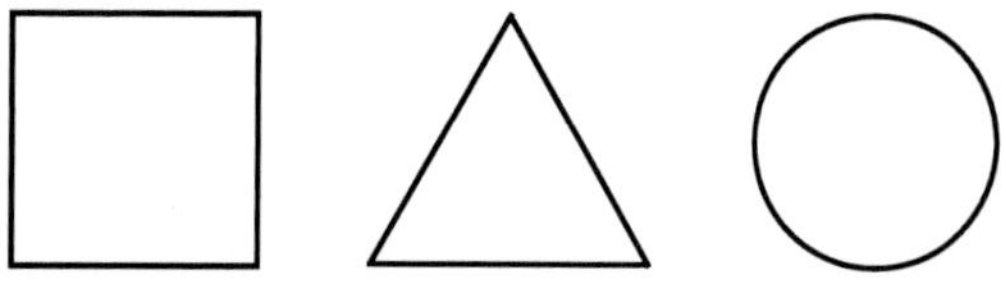

triangle circle square

Colour half of each shape.

❷ 

8 take away 4 equals ______.

❸ Colour half of these squares.

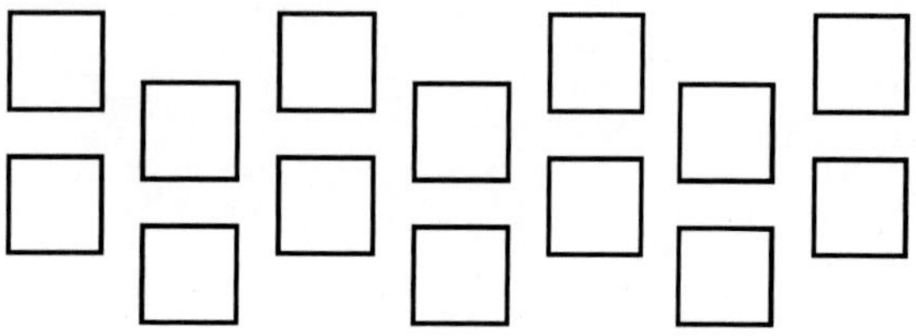

❹

$$\begin{array}{r} 6 \\ -\ 2 \\ \hline \end{array} \qquad \begin{array}{r} 8 \\ -\ 4 \\ \hline \end{array} \qquad \begin{array}{r} 9 \\ -\ 8 \\ \hline \end{array} \qquad \begin{array}{r} 7 \\ -\ 5 \\ \hline \end{array}$$

❺ 5 – 1 = ______ 7 – 1 = ______

❻ Draw a line that is parallel to each of these.

❼ What is two less than ten? ______

❽ 3 + 2 = ______

9 + 1 = ______

❾

$$\begin{array}{r} 6 \\ +\ 1 \\ \hline \end{array} \qquad \begin{array}{r} 4 \\ +\ 2 \\ \hline \end{array} \qquad \begin{array}{r} 3 \\ +\ 6 \\ \hline \end{array} \qquad \begin{array}{r} 4 \\ +\ 5 \\ \hline \end{array}$$

❿ Write the word and numeral for each.

a 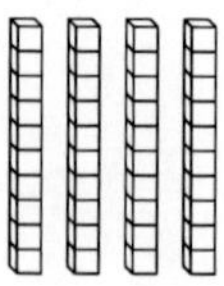 ______________ ______

b 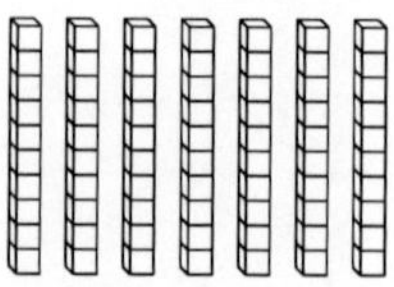 ______________ ______

c 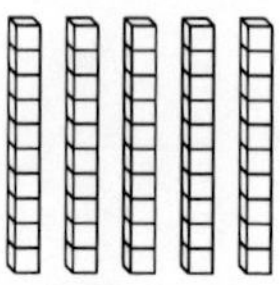 ______________ ______

d 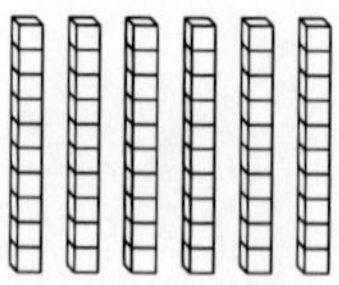 ______________ ______

 AUSTRALIAN SIGNPOST MATHS 2 MENTALS • ISBN 978 1 4886 2180 2

2:2

☐ boats

❶ Use the boats above to answer these questions.

a 10 – 2 = ____ b 10 – 4 = ____ c 10 – 7 = ____

d 10 – 5 = ____ e 10 – 3 = ____ f 10 – 10 = ____

❷ How many are in each group?

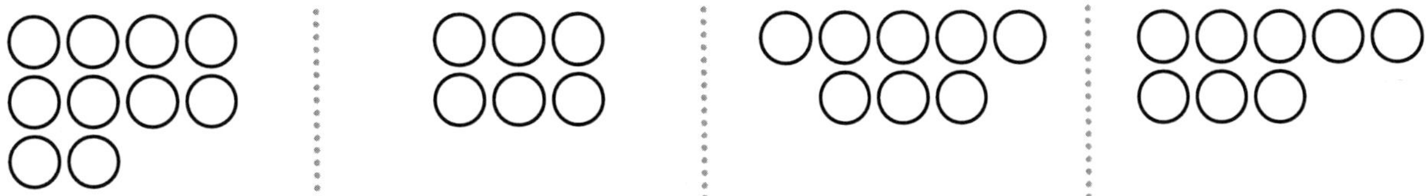

____ ____ ____ ____

Colour one half of each group of balls.

❸ What is the time?

a 

b 

c 

____ o'clock ____ o'clock ____ o'clock

2:3

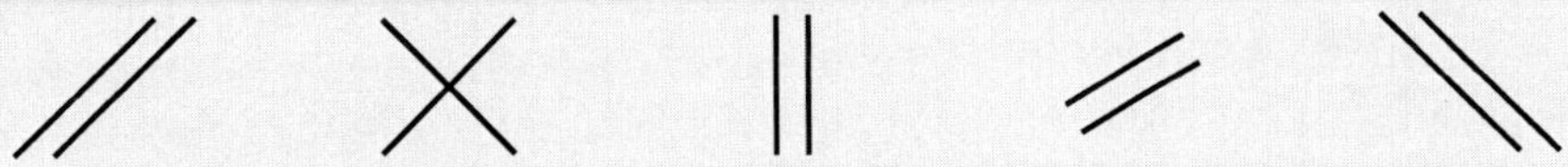

❶ a Count by 2s, starting at 1, then starting at 2.

1, 3, 5, 7, ____ 2, 4, 6, 8, ____

b Count forwards and backwards by 5s.

5, 10, 15, 20, ____ 50, 45, 40, 35, ____

c Count backwards by 2s.

19, 17, 15, 13, ____ 20, 18, 16, 14, ____

☐ Learn the days of the week and the months of the year. ☐

, ______ bones

❶

8 – ______ = ______

❷ On this clock show 7 o'clock.

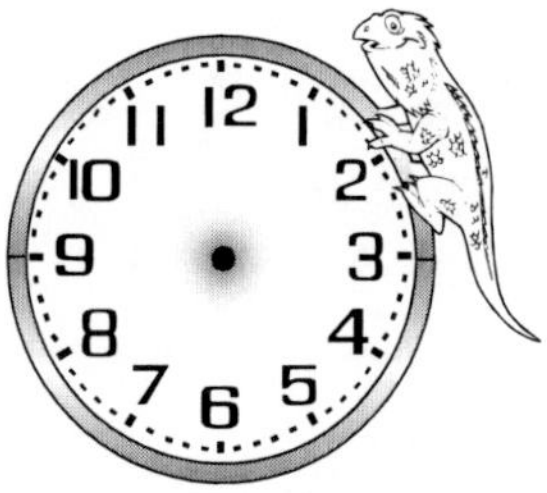

❸ Circle one half of the group.

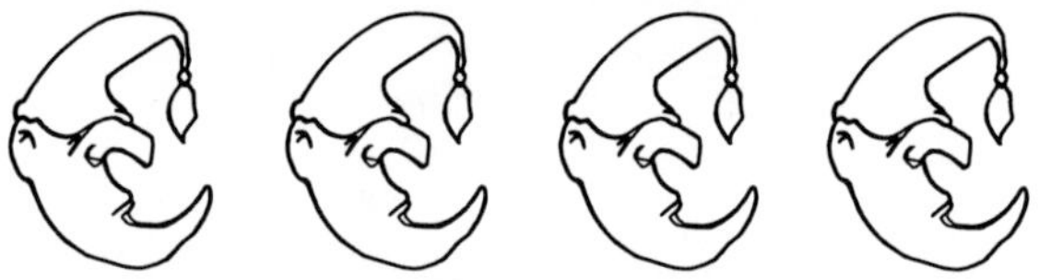

❹ Cross out the 9th flower.

❺

5	1	3
+ 3	+ 6	+ 7
___	___	___

❻

John Jim José

Who is in the middle?

____

❼ Draw a pair of parallel lines.

❽ What is the time on each clock?

half past ____ half past ____

❾ Complete each number web.

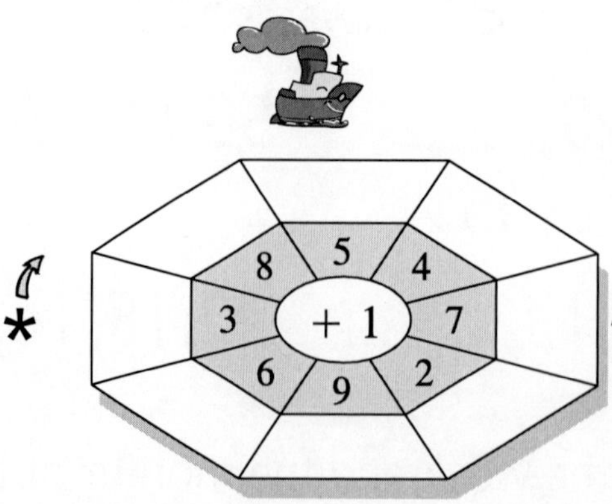

 ISBN 978 1 4886 2180 2

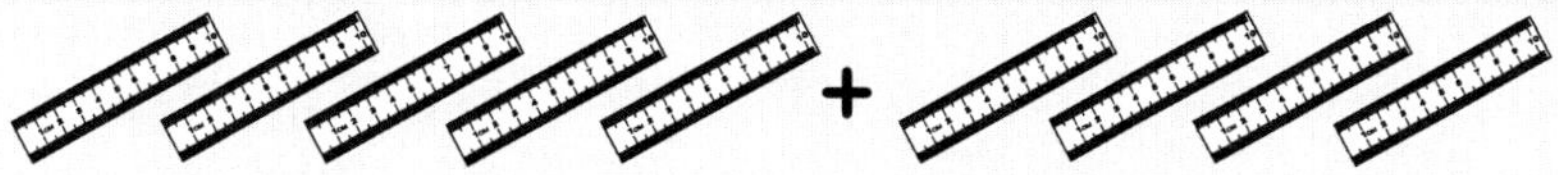

$+$, $\square + \square = \square$

❶ Colour half of each group of shapes.

a □□□□ b ○○○○○ ○○○○○ c △▽△▽△▽

❷

5	8	6	4	4
+ 2	+ 2	+ 3	+ 5	+ 3
___	___	___	___	___

❸ Name the shapes used in the picture.

____

____

____

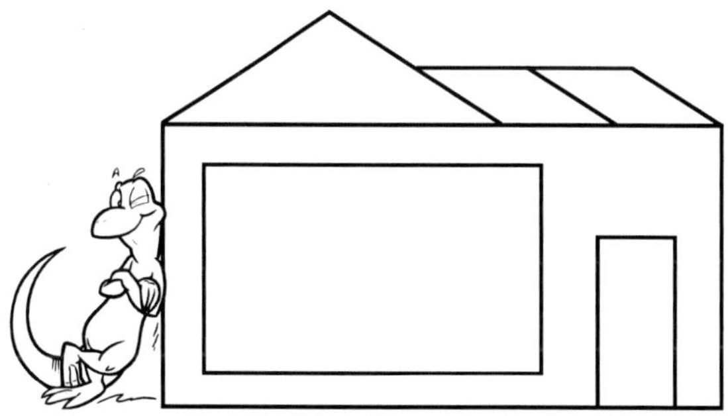

❹ Draw a girl **inside** the house.

Draw a cat **near** the house.

$+$, $\square + \square = \square$

❶ Estimate how many:

a cups of milk are in a milk carton. ______

b cartons of milk would fill a bucket. ______

c cups of milk would fill a bucket. ______

❷ How many cartons of milk would fill a bucket if a carton holds 4 cups of milk and 40 cups of milk fill a bucket? ______

How many butterflies? □

1. Continue this pattern.

   40, 45, 50, ____ , ____

2. How many sides on each shape?

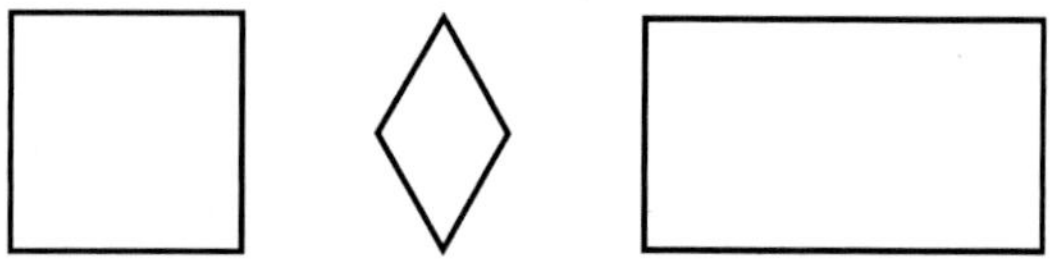

____ ____ ____

Draw 2 lines to cut each shape in quarters.

Colour one quarter of each.

3. 9 – 3 = ____

   7 – 4 = ____

4. Circle the object you would use to fill a bucket.

5. 2, 4, 6, ____ , 10, ____ , 14

6. Name each coin.

____ ____

____ ____

7. Circle the shapes you can stack.

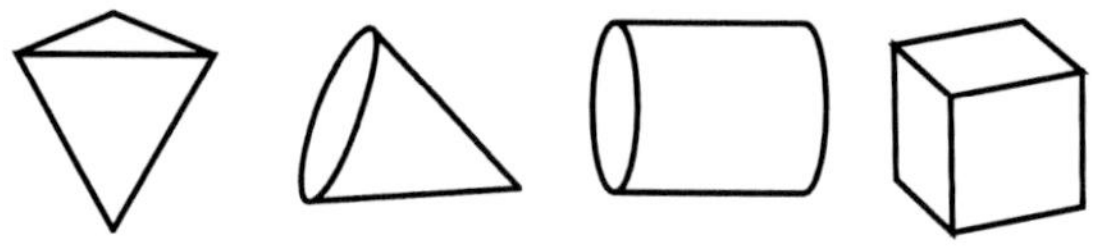

8. A B C D

Which holds the most?

____

9. Show the time on each clock.

9 o'clock

9 : 00

When it is o'clock, the big hand points to 12.

a

4 o'clock

4 : 00

b

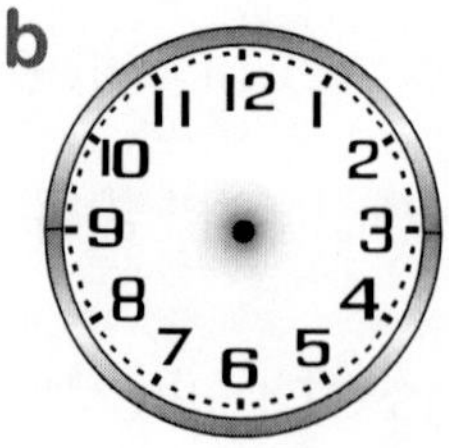

6 o'clock

6 : 00

c

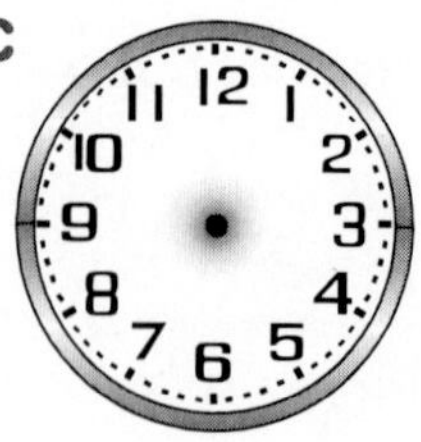

1 o'clock

1 : 00

 ISBN 978 1 4886 2180 2

4:2

1. Write the number one more than: 67 ____ 49 ____ 60 ____

2. Show the times on these clocks:

:	:	:	:
6 o'clock	half past 3	4 thirty	half past 9

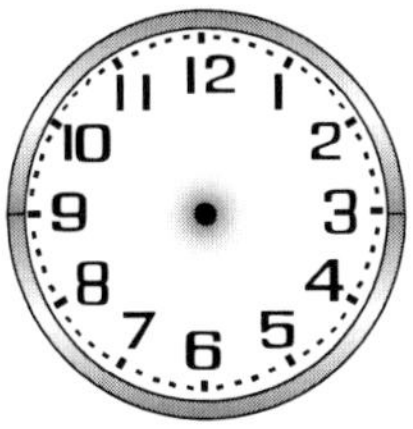 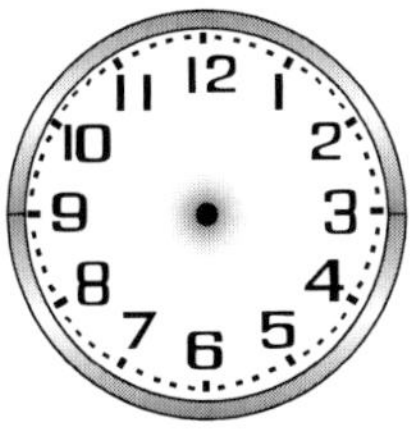  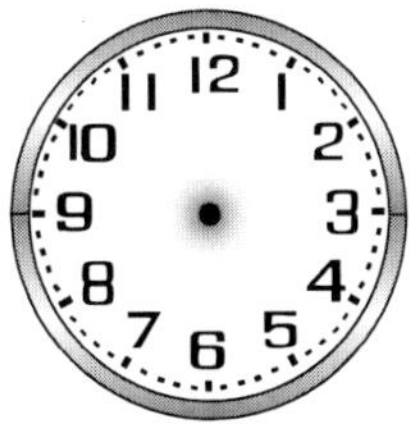

4:3

30, 35, 40, 45, 50, 55, 60, ____, ____, ____

1. a Count backwards by twos from 100.

   100, ____, ____, ____, ____, ____, ____

   b Count backwards by tens from 100.

   100, ____, ____, ____, ____, ____, ____

   c Count backwards by fives from 100.

   100, ____, ____, ____, ____, ____, ____

21	22	23	24	25	26	27	28	29	30
31	32	33	34	35	36	37	38	39	40
41	42	43	44	45	46	47	48	49	50
51	52	53	54	55	56	57	58	59	60
61	62	63	64	65	66	67	68	69	70
71	72	73	74	75	76	77	78	79	80
81	82	83	84	85	86	87	88	89	90
91	92	93	94	95	96	97	98	99	100

   d Count backwards by twos from 79.

   79, ____, ____, ____, ____, ____, ____, ____, ____

   e Count backwards by tens from 89.

   89, ____, ____, ____, ____, ____, ____, ____, ____

☐ groups of ten dogs = ☐

5:1

, □ – □ = □

❶ 8 – 3 = ______

8 – 5 = ______

❷ Circle the objects that can roll.

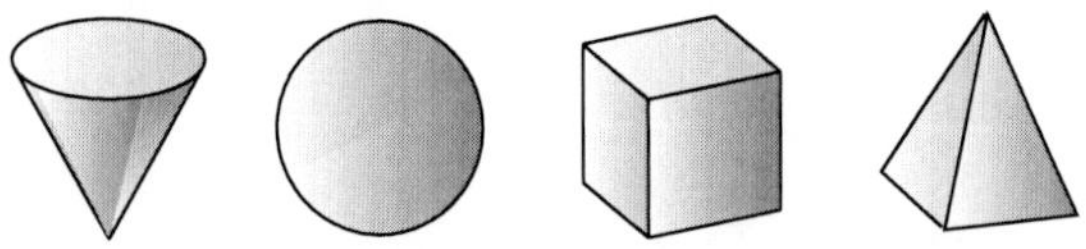

❸ Draw something that would balance the orange.

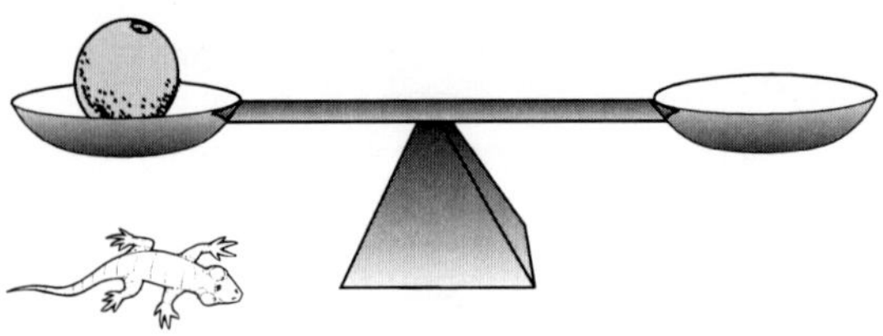

❹ ______ + ______ = 20

______ + ______ + ______ = 10

❺ Write the numeral for:

eleven _____ fourteen _____

❻ Draw lines to cut each object in quarters. Colour $\frac{1}{4}$.

❼

4	1	4	5
+ 1	+ 7	+ 6	+ 5
____	____	____	____

❽ Circle the objects that have curved surfaces.

❾ Circle the container that holds more than a jug.

❿ Place-value blocks

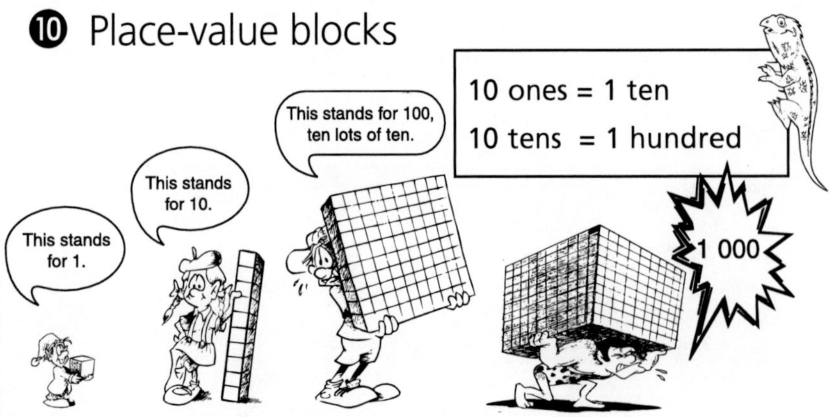

a 20 ones = ______ tens

b 30 ones = ______ tens

c 2 hundreds

= ______ tens

5:2

 + , ☐ + ☐ = ☐

❶ Write the number **after**:

a 119 ____ b 131 ____ c 127 ____

❷ Write the number **before**:

a ____ 117 b ____ 130 c ____ 103

71	72	73	74	75	76	77	78	79	80
81	82	83	84	85	86	87	88	89	90
91	92	93	94	95	96	97	98	99	100
101	102	103	104	105	106	107	108	109	110
111	112	113	114	115	116	117	118	119	120
121	122	123	124	125	126	127	128	129	130
131	132	133	134	135	136	137	138	139	140

❸ a Count by 2s from 73.

73, ____, ____, ____, ____

b Count by 10s from 79.

79, ____, ____, ____, ____

c Count by 5s from 82.

82, ____, ____, ____, ____

d Count by 10s from 93.

93, ____, ____, ____, ____

❹  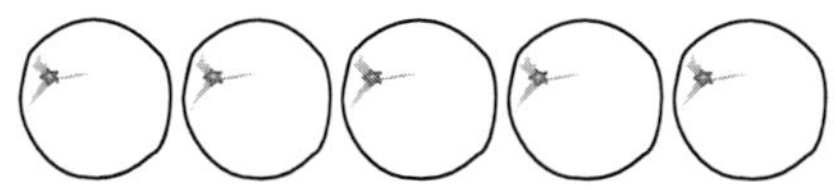

How many more apples are there than oranges? ____

5:3

 + , ☐ + ☐ = ☐

5 + 2 = ☐ We say: 5…6…7, so 5 and 2 make 7.

❶ a 8 + 2 = ____ b 11 + 2 = ____ c 15 + 2 = ____

d 12 + 3 = ____ e 17 + 3 = ____ f 16 + 3 = ____

g 23 + 1 = ____ h 27 + 2 = ____ i 25 + 3 = ____

How many stars? ☐

6:1

 , ☐ − ☐ = ☐

❶ What number is modelled?

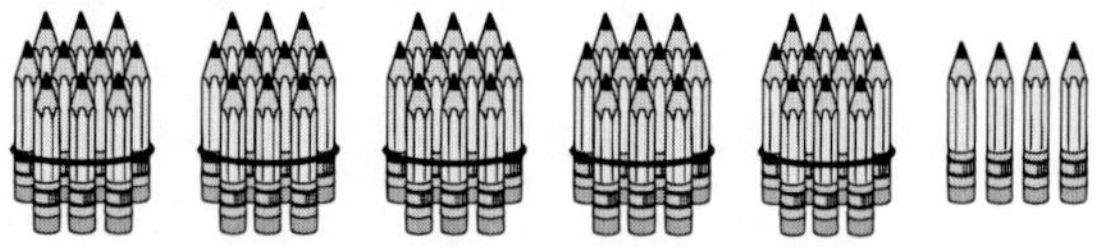

_____ tens _____ ones = _____

❷ This is a ________________.

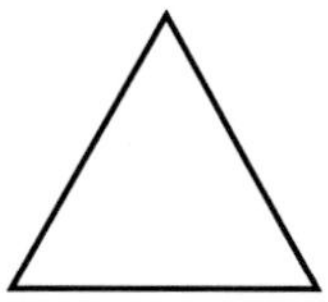

_____ sides

_____ corners

❸ Double 6 = _____

6 + 6 = _____

6 + 5 = _____

6 + 7 = _____

❹ 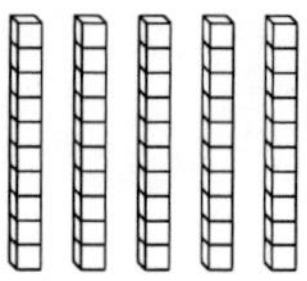

| ☐ | Tens | = _____

❺ _____ + _____ = 13

_____ + _____ + _____ = 8

❻ Trace the shortest way for the bird to reach the tree.

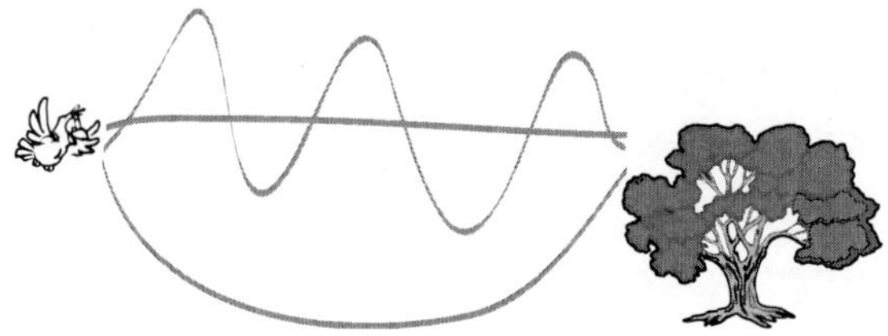

❼ Circle the animal with the smallest mass and colour the one with the greatest mass.

❽ 36, 37, ___, ___, 40

❾ Complete each number web.

*

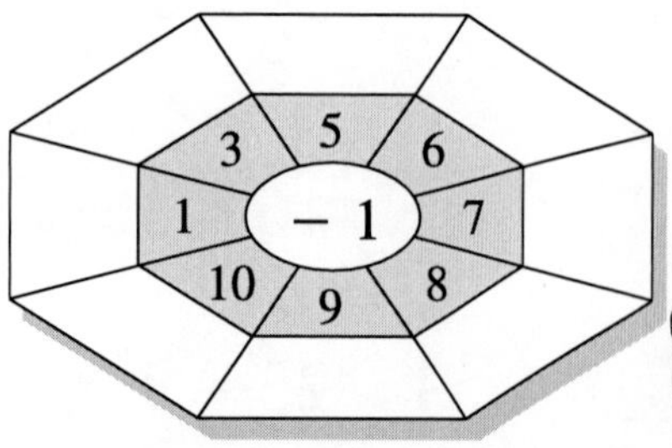

*

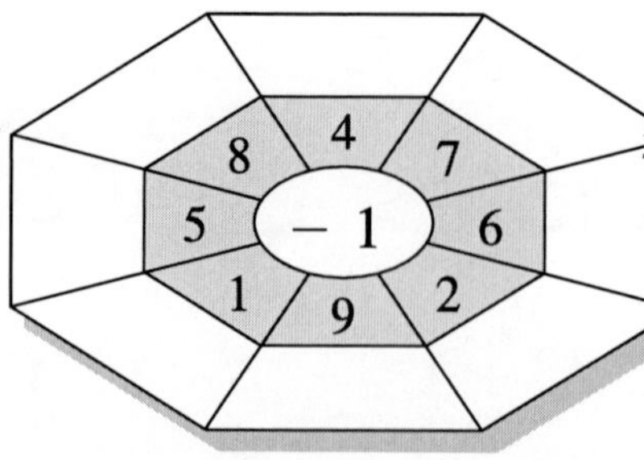

6:2 Monday Tuesday Wednesday Thursday Friday

❶ 

9	6	10	9	7
+ 5	+ 8	+ 7	+ 8	+ 6
____	____	____	____	____

❷ 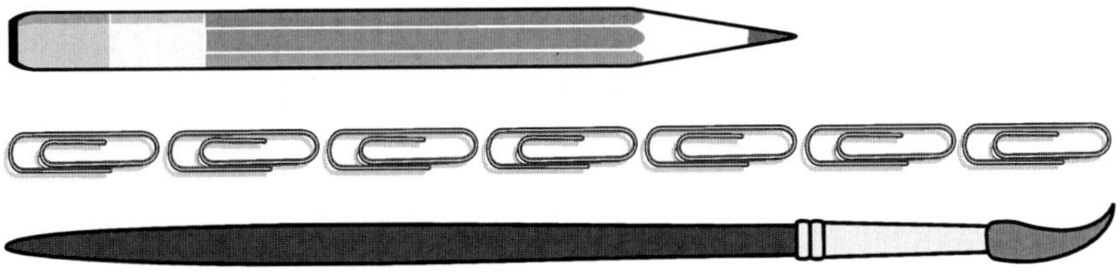

a How long is the pencil?

______ paperclips

b How long is the paintbrush?

______ paperclips

6:3

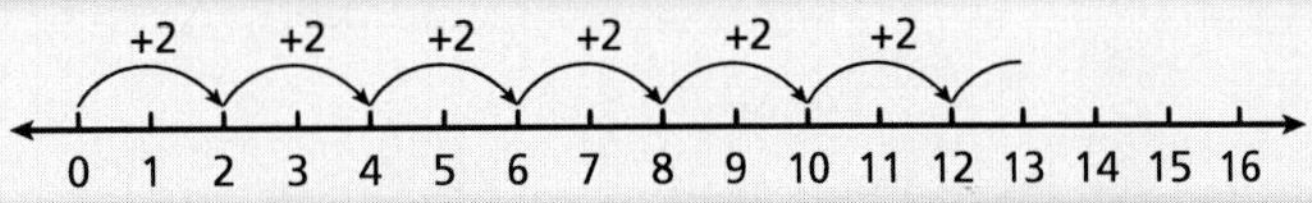

❶ Continue each pattern.

a 2, 4, 6, 8, ____, ____, ____, ____

b 22, 24, 26, ____, ____, ____, ____

c 5, 10, 15, ____, ____, ____, ____

d 10, 20, 30, ____, ____, ____, ____

e 100, 110, 120, ____, ____, ____

☐ groups of ten dots = ☐

5, 10, 15, 20, 25, 30, ___, ___, ___

1 Double 5 = ______

5 + 5 = ______

5 + 6 = ______

5 + 4 = ______

2 

______ rows of ______ = ______

3 This time is: 

____

4 Circle the taller building.

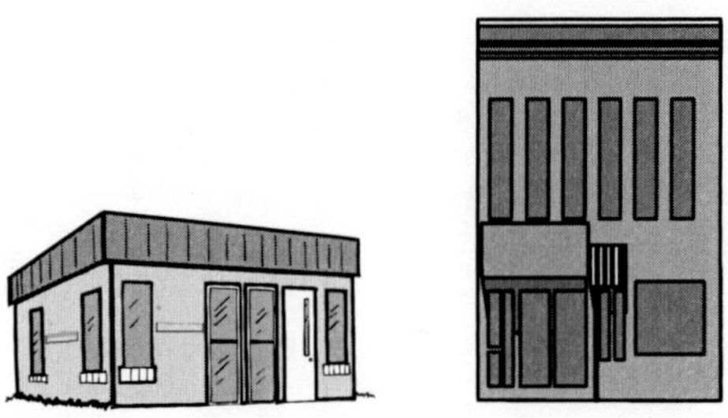

5 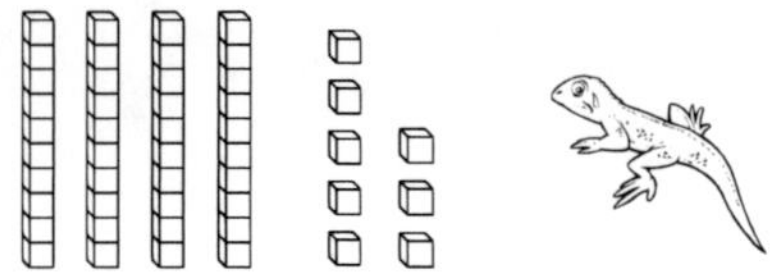

______ tens ______ ones = ______

6 How many ones blocks make one tens block? ______

How many ones blocks make two tens blocks? ______

7 Estimate how many craft sticks will be needed to measure the length of your desk.

______ craft sticks

8 Write the numerals for:

forty ______ sixty ______

9 This time is:

____

10 **a** 

How many dogs? ☐ How many more dogs than rabbits? ☐

b 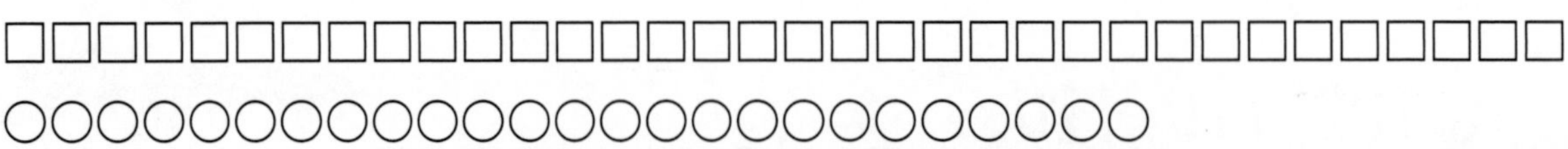

How many squares? ☐ How many more squares than circles? ☐

7:2

 –  = ☐

❶ Draw a line to join each shape to its name.

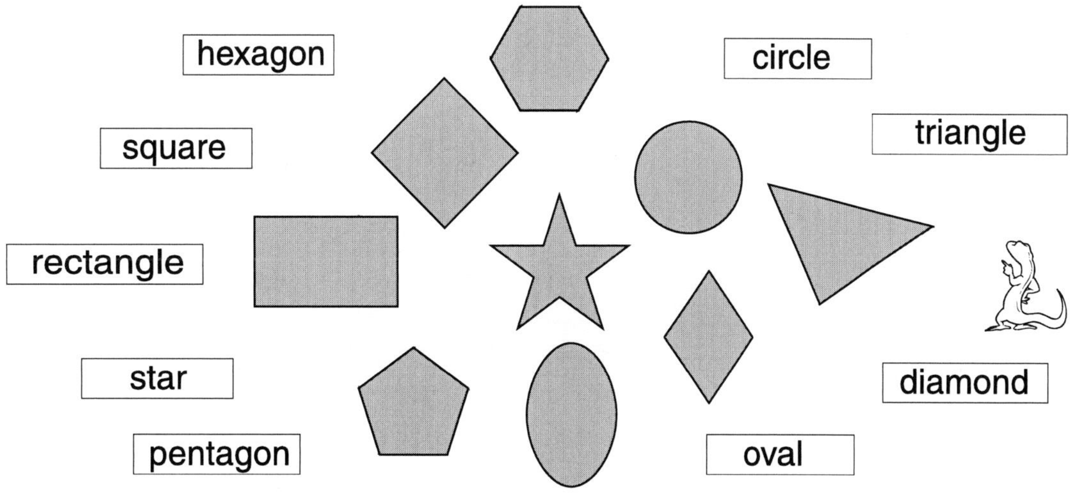

❷ Continue these patterns.

a 36, 37, 38, ___, ___

b 22, 21, 20, ___, ___

c 10, 20, 30, ___, ___

d 2, 4, 6, ___, ___

7:3

 = ☐

❶ The pattern continues on the 4th picture.

a Find how the tiles change. Shade the grey tiles in the 4th picture.

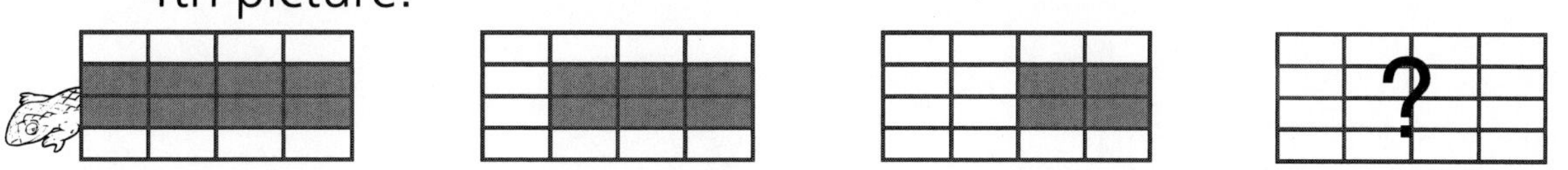

8 grey tiles	___ grey tiles	___ grey tiles	___ grey tiles
8 white tiles	___ white tiles	___ white tiles	___ white tiles

b How many grey tiles would be used altogether? ______

c How many white tiles would be used altogether? ______

How many elephants? ☐

8:1

1:00 ______ o'clock, 4:00 ______ o'clock

❶ Double 8 = ______

8 + 8 = ______

8 + 7 = ______

8 + 9 = ______

❷ Draw stars to make equal groups.

______ groups of ______ = ______

❸

______ + ______ = ______

❹ Write the number two after:

a 87 ____ **b** 49 ____

❺ This time is:

______

❻ Share 15 counters among 3 girls.

Each girl is given ______ counters.

❼ Write the numerals for:

eighteen ______

fourteen ______

❽

______ rows of ______

= ______

❾ Complete each number web.

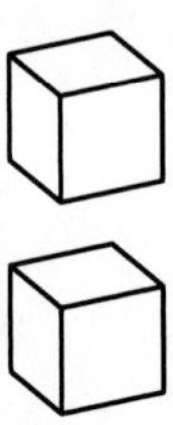

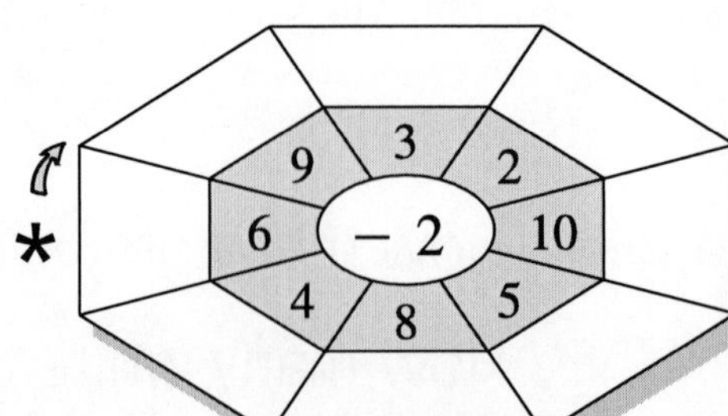

 • *AUSTRALIAN SIGNPOST MATHS 2 MENTALS* • ISBN 978 1 4886 2180 2

8:2

❶ 

_____ rows of _____

= _____

❷ 

_____ groups of _____

= _____

❸ a How many green pencils? _____

b How many yellow pencils? _____

c How many more blue than green? _____

d How many altogether? _____

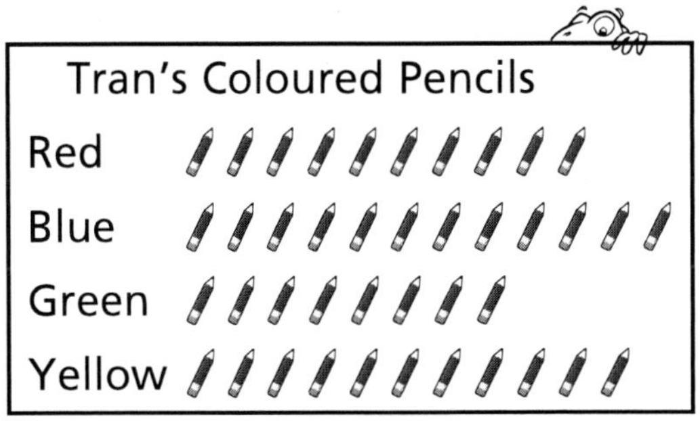

8:3

❶ Draw a line to cut each shape in half.
Colour $\frac{1}{2}$ of each shape.

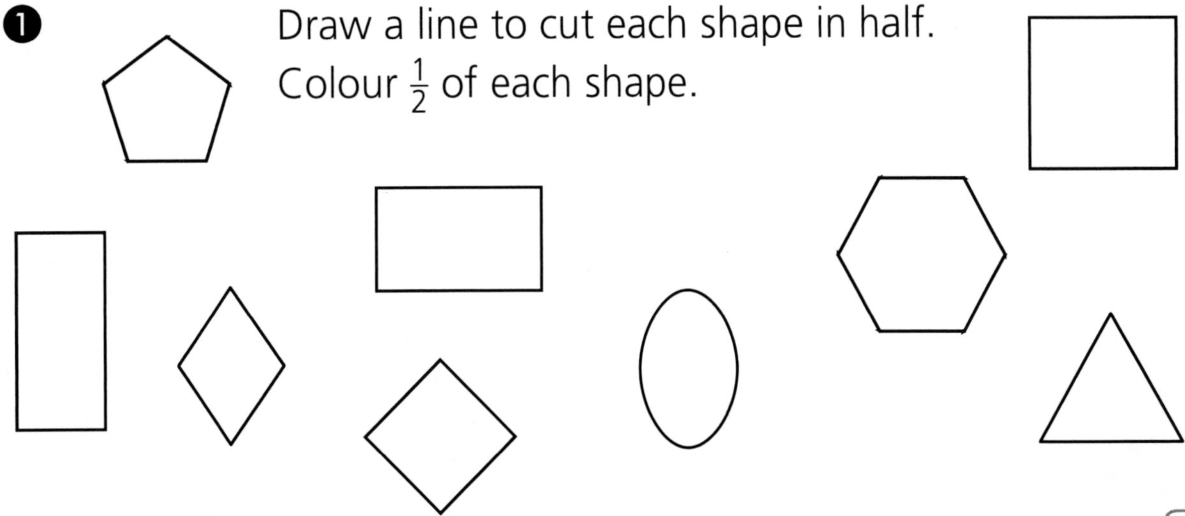

How many tops? ☐

9:1  , ☐ **groups of** ☐ **=** ☐

❶ Write the numerals.

thirty ______ fifty ______

❷ 8 + 2 = ____ 7 + 2 = ____

❸ 17 cars. ☐

5 lost. – ☐

How many left? ☐

❹ Share 6 lollies between 2 children.

☐ ☐

How many lollies each? ______

❺ Colour half of each group.

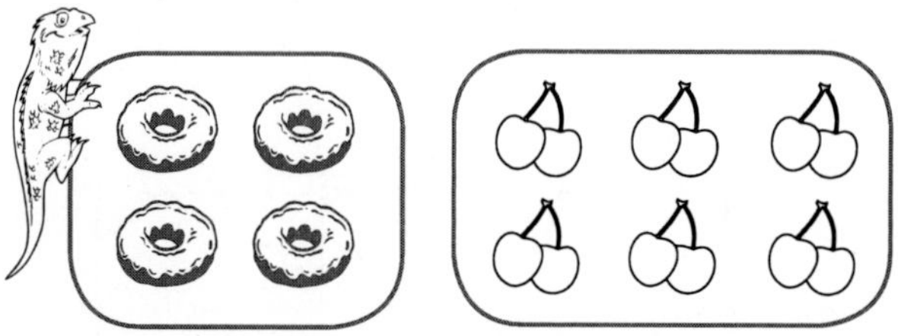

❻ 

____ groups of ____ = ____

____ × ____ = ____

❼

12	18	14
– 9	– 3	– 5
____	____	____

❽ Show a quarter past 5 on the clock.

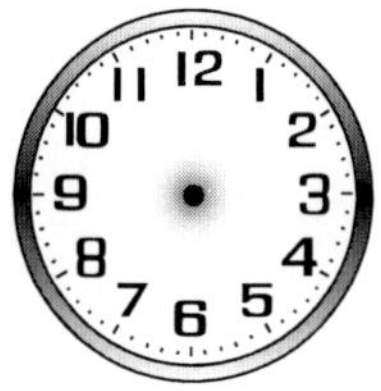

❾ Colour a quarter of each group.

❿ Write 3 different number sentences.

____ + ____ + ____ =

____ + ____ + ____ = **14**

____ + ____ + ____ =

⓫ Complete each number web.

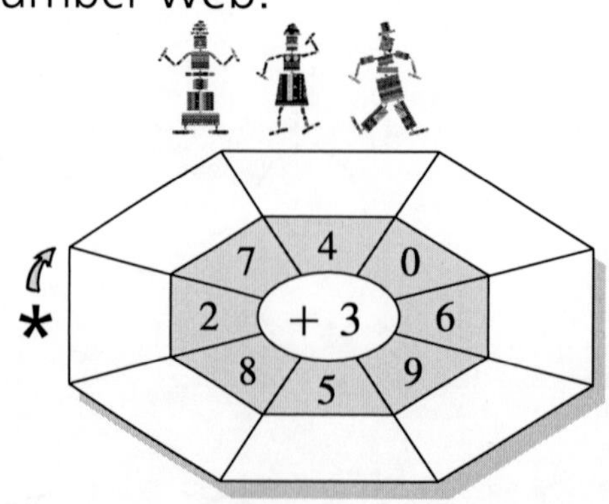

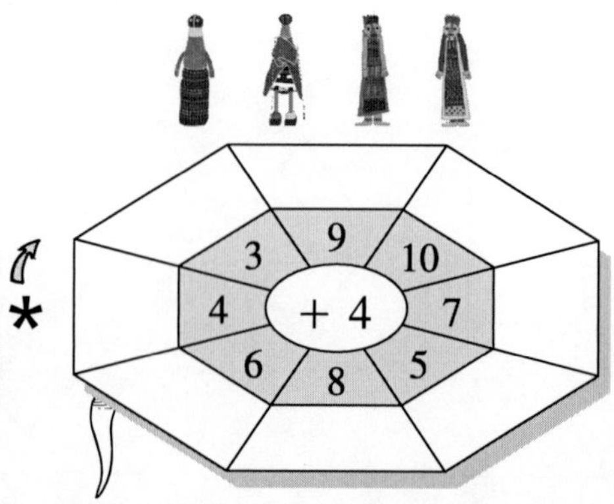

 ISBN 978 1 4886 2180 2

9:2

1

Circles	● ● ● ● ● ● ● ● ● ● ● ● ● ● ● ● ● ●
Squares	■ ■
Triangles	▲ ▲ ▲ ▲ ▲ ▲ ▲ ▲ ▲ ▲ ▲ ▲ ▲ ▲ ▲ ▲

a How many circles and triangles altogether? ______

b How many more squares than circles? ______

c How many more circles than triangles? ______

d How many shapes altogether? ______

2 Circle the widest crown.

3 Circle the wider bottle.

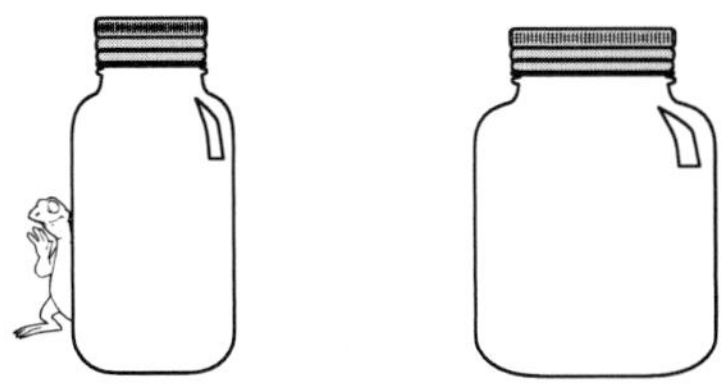

9:3

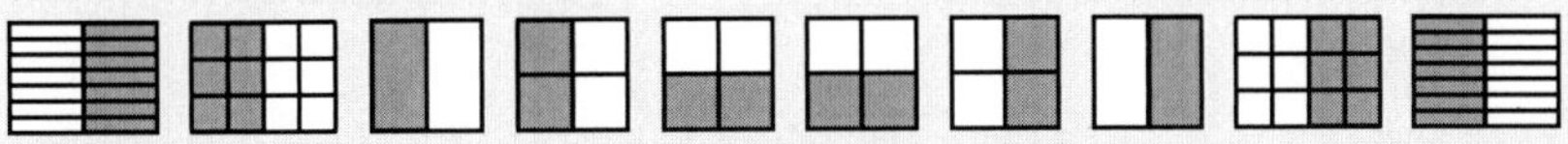

1 Colour half of each shape.

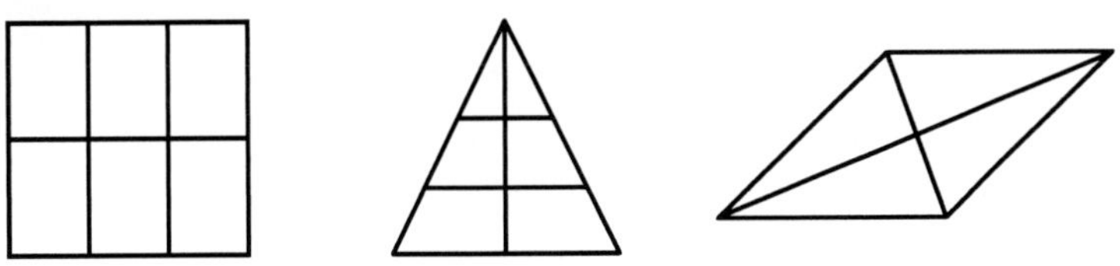

2 Colour a quarter of each shape.

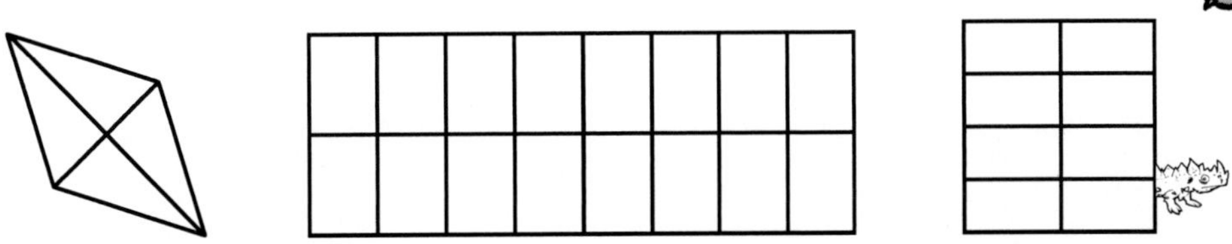

☐ groups of ☐ balls = ☐

 , ☐ – ☐ = ☐

❶ 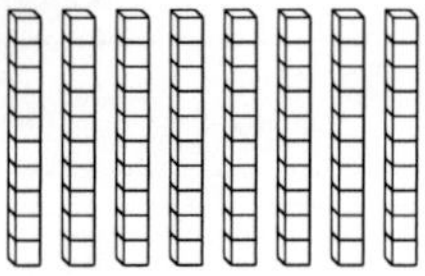

= ______ tens
= eighty
= ______

❷ Write the number after:

a 421 ______ b 296 ______

c 839 ______ d 567 ______

❸ Write the number of corners on the shapes.

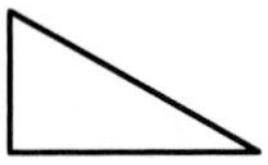 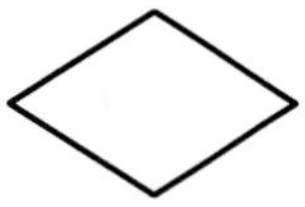

______ ______

❹ 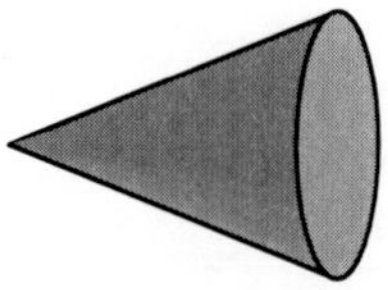

Is this object pointed? ______

❺ 19 cakes.

5 eaten. –

How many now?

❻ Write 3 different number sentences.

____ + ____ + ____ =
____ + ____ + ____ = 17
____ + ____ + ____ =

❼ Circle one quarter of this group.

❽ Write the number modelled.

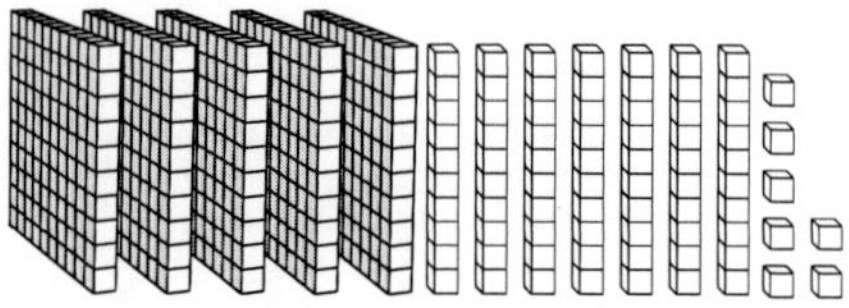

______

❾ This is a ______________.

It has ________ sides.

It has ________ corners.

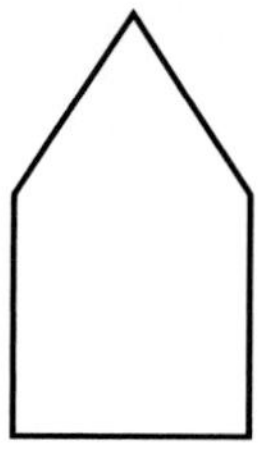

❿ 17 – 10 = ______

17 – 7 = ______

⓫ Complete each number web.

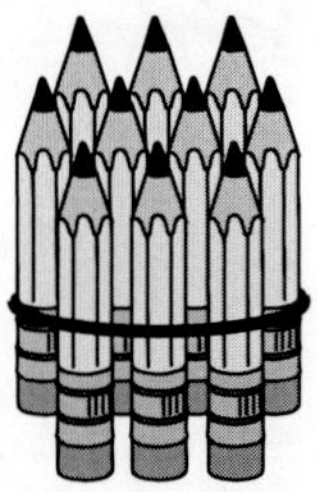

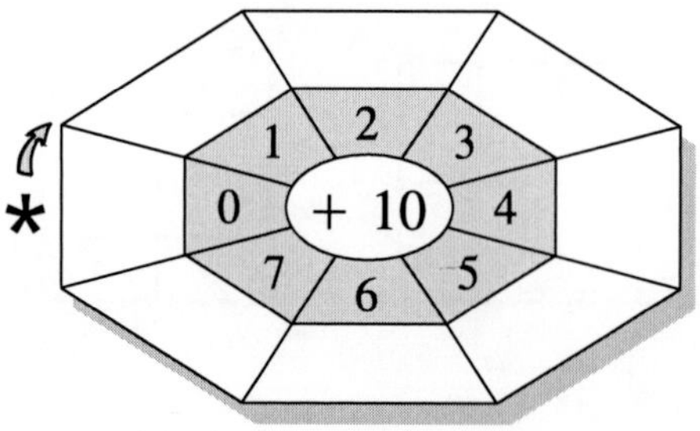

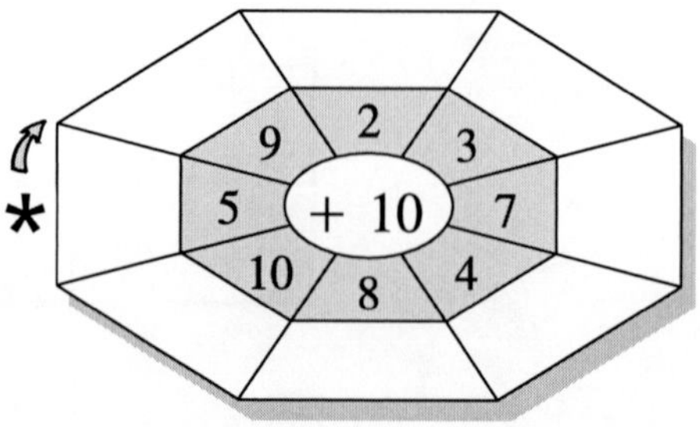

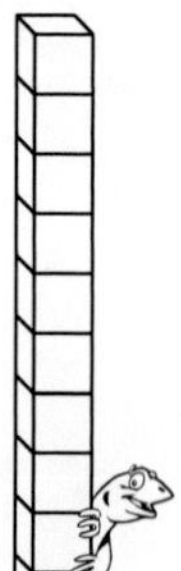

© PEARSON AUSTRALIA 2018 • *AUSTRALIAN SIGNPOST MATHS 2 MENTALS* • ISBN 978 1 4886 2180 2

10:2 1st, 2nd, 3rd, 4th, 5th, 6th, 7th, 8th, 9th, ________

❶ Colour one face on each 3D object.

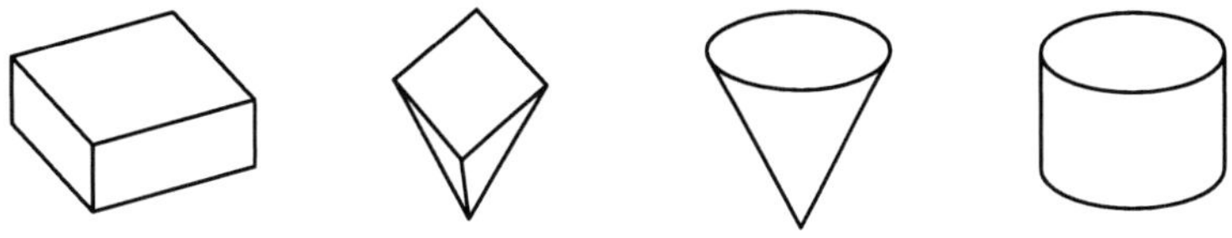

❷ Circle the pictures that show halves.
Tick the picture that shows quarters.

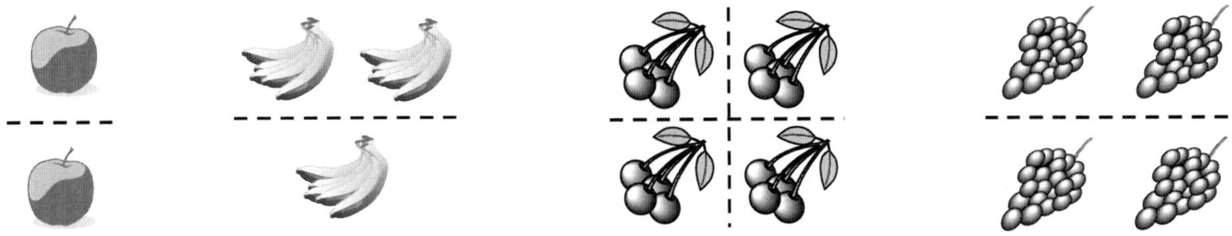

❸

18	14	19	17	16
– 9	– 6	– 10	– 8	– 5
____	____	____	____	____

10:3

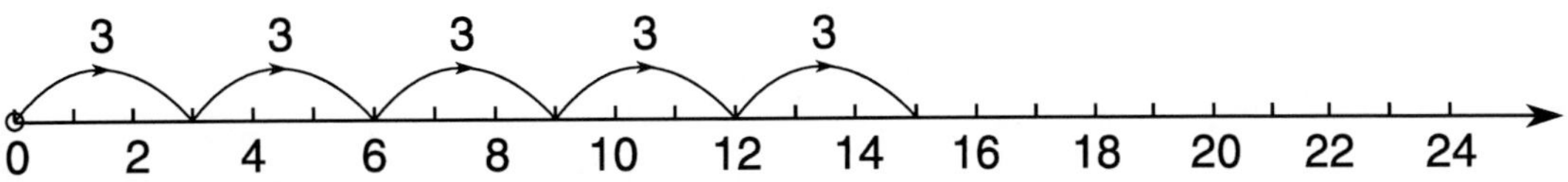

❹ We can use a number line to find **groups of** or **rows of**.
5 groups of 3 = 15.

a 3 groups of 3 = ______

b 4 rows of 3 = ______

c 4 groups of 2 = ______

d 8 rows of 2 = ______

e 7 groups of 3 = ______

f 6 rows of 4 = ______

☐ groups of eight cows = ☐

 , ☐ × ☐ = ☐

❶ 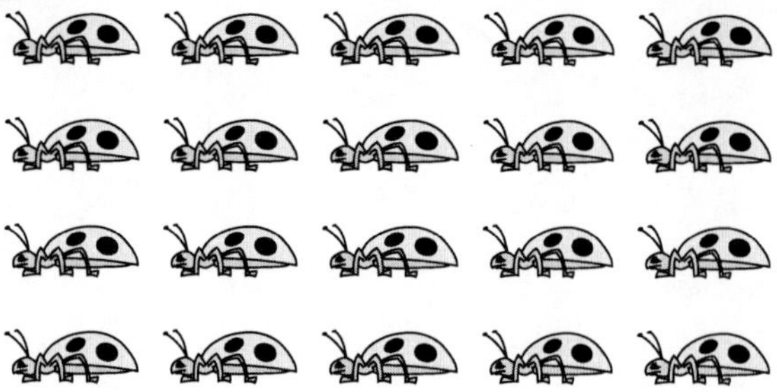

_____ rows of _____ = _____

_____ × _____ = _____

❷ Circle half the ladybugs.

❸ ☆☆☆☆☆☆☆☆☆☆☆☆☆

13 altogether. ☐

4 given away. − ☐

How many left? ☐

❹ Circle the shape with the greater area.

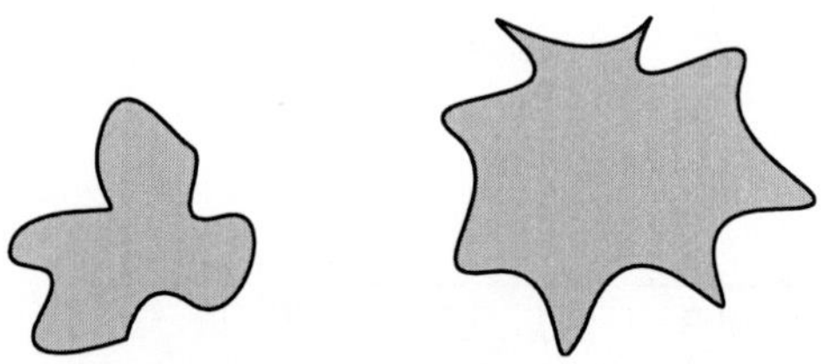

❺ 12 − 6 = _____

11 − 6 = _____

❻ Write the number of angles on these shapes.

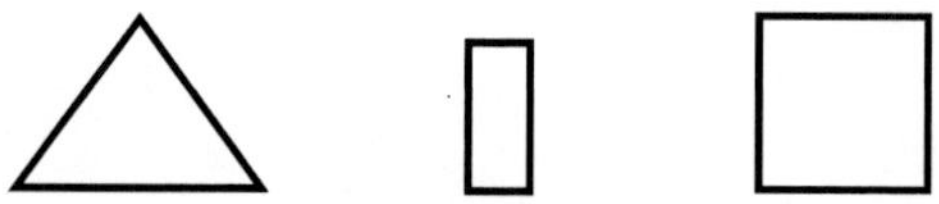

_____ _____ _____

❼ Circle: It is **likely / unlikely** that a lion will be in your classroom this week.

❽ 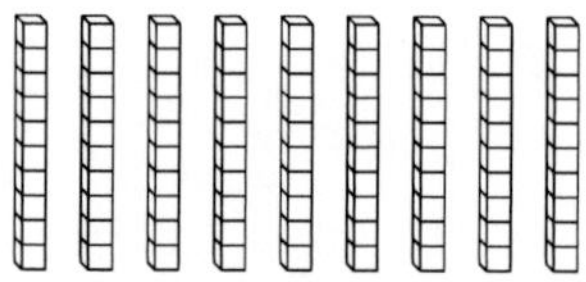

	Tens

= _____

❾ Complete this number pattern.

34, 35, 36, _____, _____, _____

❿ 70 = _____ tens _____ ones

⓫ Write the numbers modelled.

a 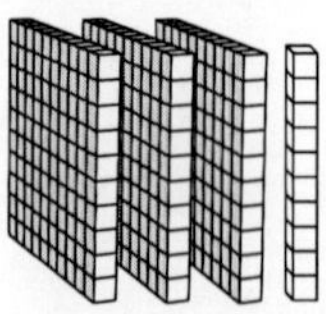 _____

b 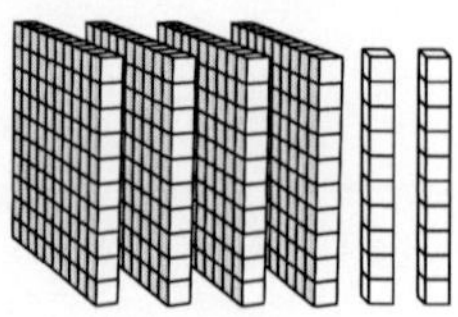 _____

c 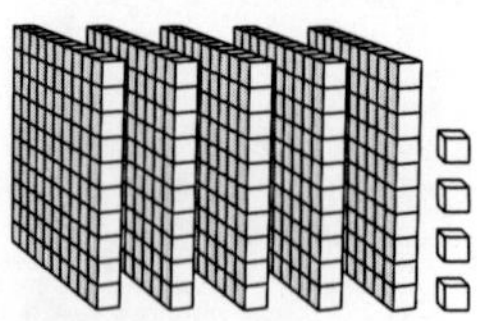 _____

d  _____

e  _____

11:2

3 groups of 3 = ☐

❶ Circle the groups that are divided into quarters.

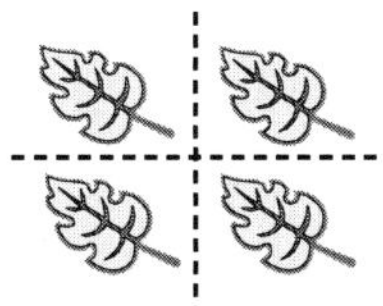

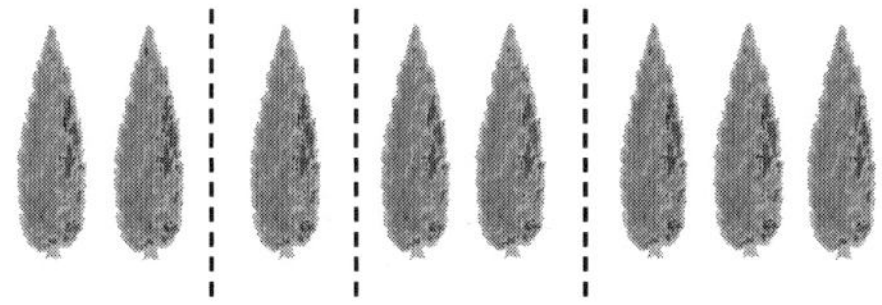

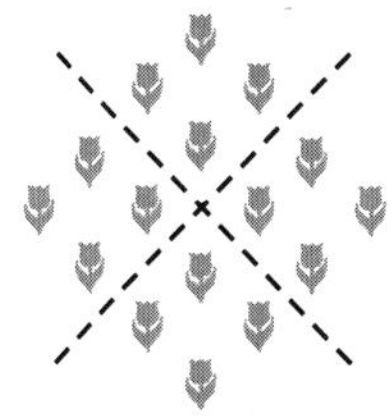

❷ Circle the shapes that have only flat surfaces.

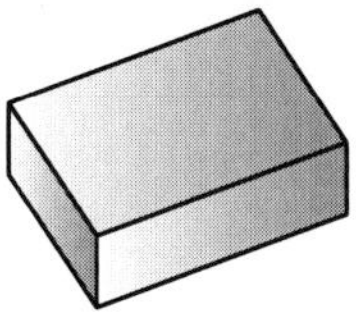

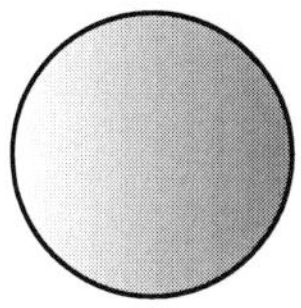

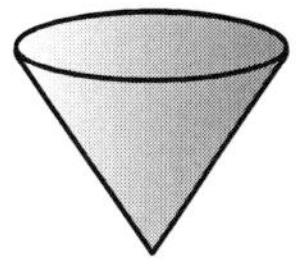

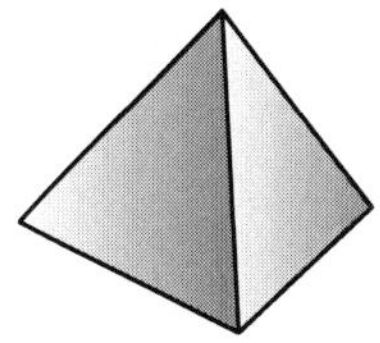

❸ Draw 3 groups of 5 balls.

3 groups of 5 = ______ $3 \times 5 =$ ______

11:3

❹ Write the missing numbers in each pattern then write the rule.

a 10, 20, ____, 40, ____, ____, 70 Rule ____________

b 4, 14, ____, 34, 44, ____, 64 Rule ____________

c 7, 17, 27, ____, 47, 57, ____ Rule ____________

d 21, ____, 41, 51, ____, 71, 81 Rule ____________

 • • ISBN 978 1 4886 2180 2

❶ 16 – 2 = ______

15 – 2 = ______

❷ Complete the cone.

How many:

corners? ______

edges? ______

surfaces? ______

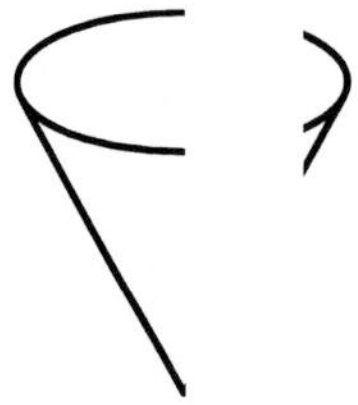

❸ Draw three groups of two flowers.

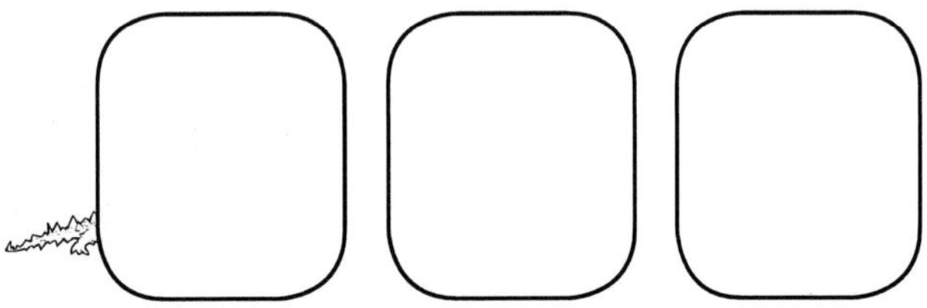

_____ groups of _____ = _____

_____ × _____ = _____

❹ This is a c __________.

Its ends are circles and it has one curved surface.

❺ Write the number modelled.

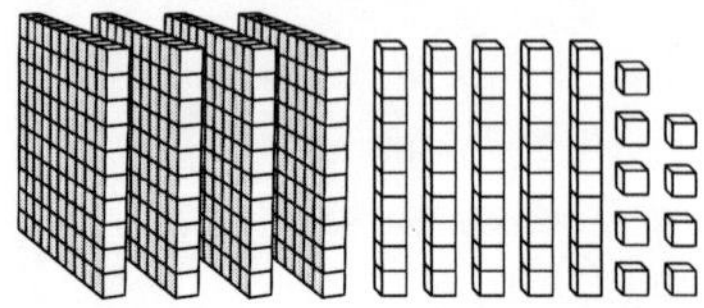

______

❻ Double 4.

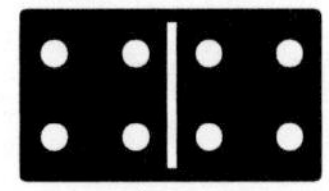

______ + ______ = ______

2 × 4 = ______

❼ Write something that is impossible to happen.

____

❽ Colour the mat with the larger area.

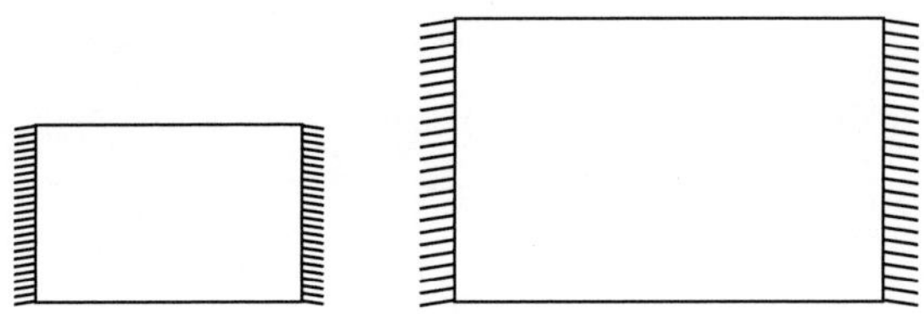

❾ 10 + 3 = ______

10 + 7 = ______

❿ Complete each number web.

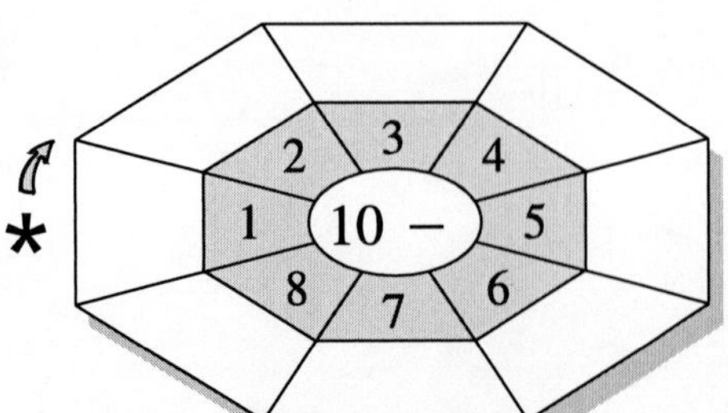

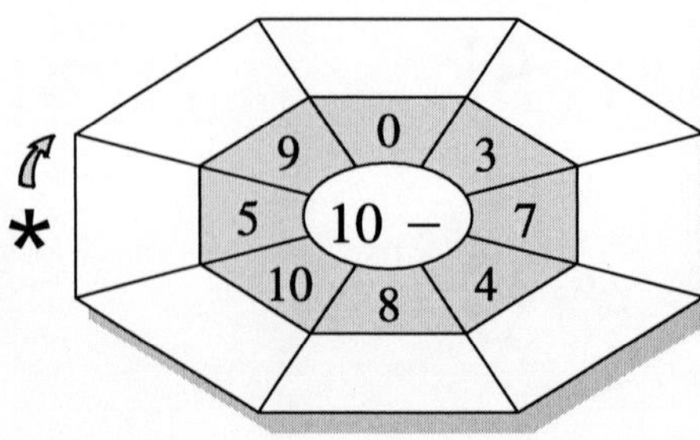

© PEARSON AUSTRALIA 2018 • *AUSTRALIAN SIGNPOST MATHS 2 MENTALS* • ISBN 978 1 4886 2180 2

12:2

, ☐ - ☐ = ☐

❶ Colour one half of each shape.

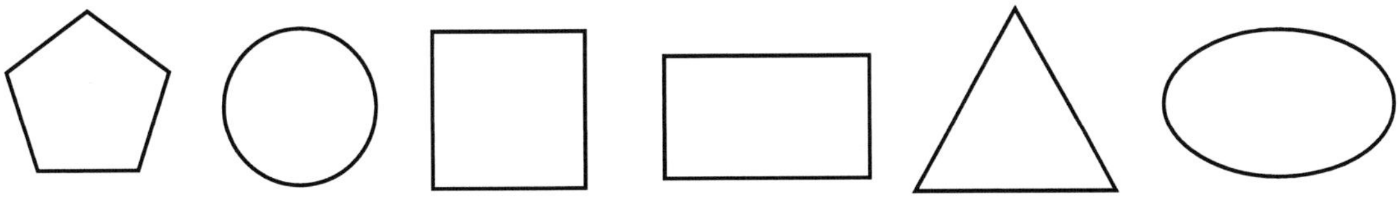

❷ **a** 30 = ____ tens **b** 70 = ____ tens **c** 90 = ____ tens

❸ Colour the **1st** car red.

Put a cross on the **10th** car.

Circle the **7th** car.

12:3

= ☐

❶ We can use a number line to add numbers. 5 + 6 + 9 = 20

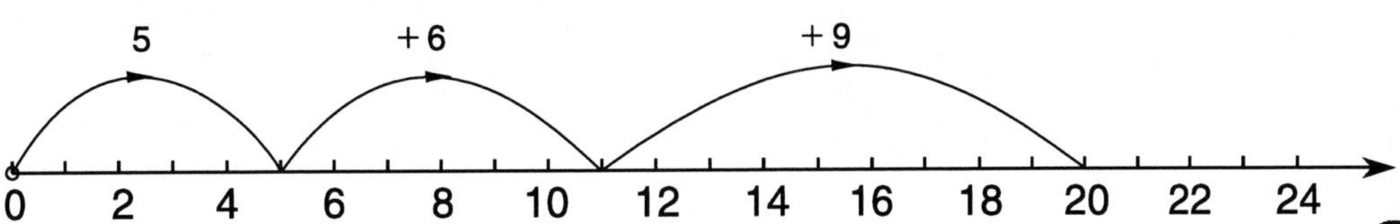

a 3 + 3 + 7 = ______ **b** 10 + 7 + 5 = ______

c 9 + 3 + 8 = ______ **d** 14 + 6 + 3 = ______

e 7 + 9 + 6 = ______ **f** 12 + 7 + 4 = ______

How many seals? ☐

 • *AUSTRALIAN SIGNPOST MATHS 2 MENTALS* • ISBN 978 1 4886 2180 2

13:1

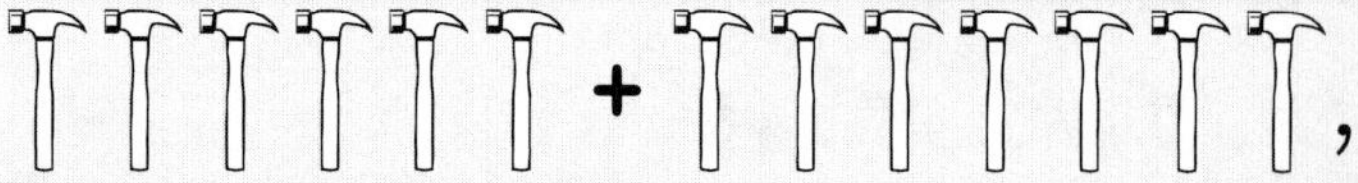
, ☐ + ☐ = ☐

❶ 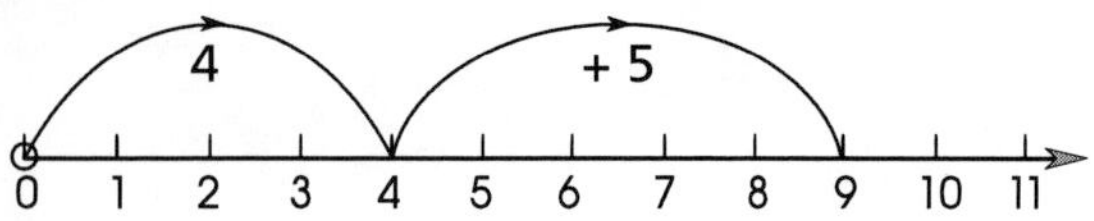

4 + 5 = ______

❷ 11 – 8 = ______

11 – 3 = ______

❸ Share 6 counters between the 3 boxes.

❹ Draw more lollies to make four fair shares.

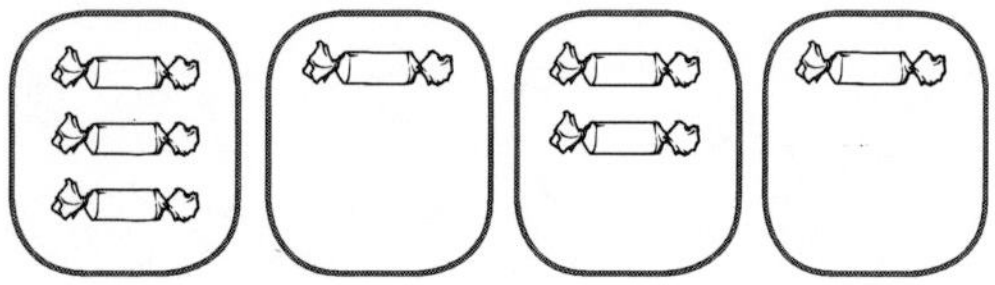

4 groups of 3 = ______

❺ 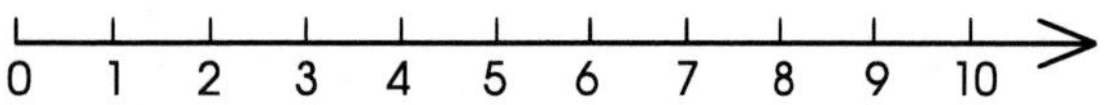

This is a n ______________

l ______________.

❻ **a** How many groups? ______

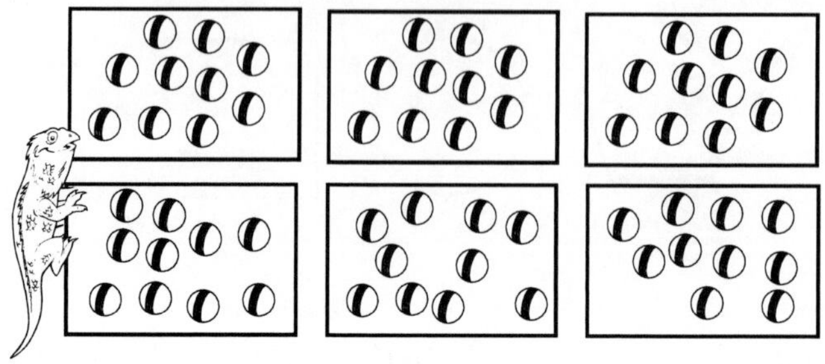

b How many in each group? ______

c How many balls? ______

❼ Complete the cylinder.

How many:

corners? ______

edges? ______

surfaces? ______

❽ 

______ rows of ______ = ______

______ × ______ = ______

❾ 

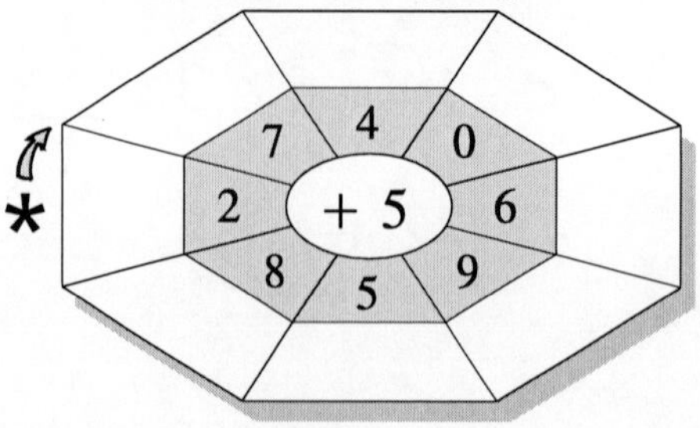

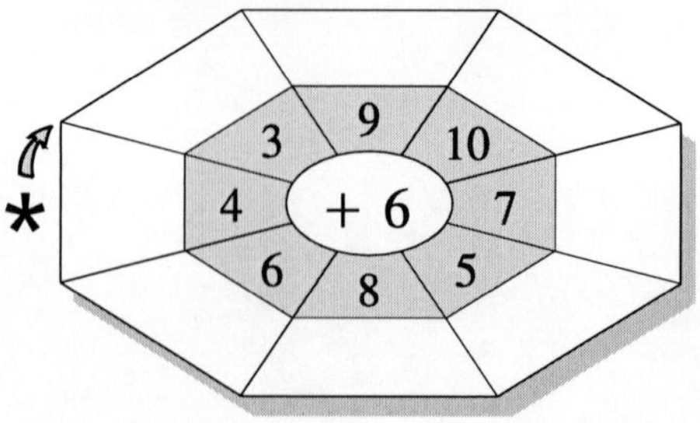

© PEARSON AUSTRALIA 2018 • *AUSTRALIAN SIGNPOST MATHS 2 MENTALS* • ISBN 978 1 4886 2180 2

13:2

, ☐ **groups of** ☐ **=** ☐

❶ Three girls shared these dogs. How many each? ______

❷ Draw lines to match each fraction picture with a word.

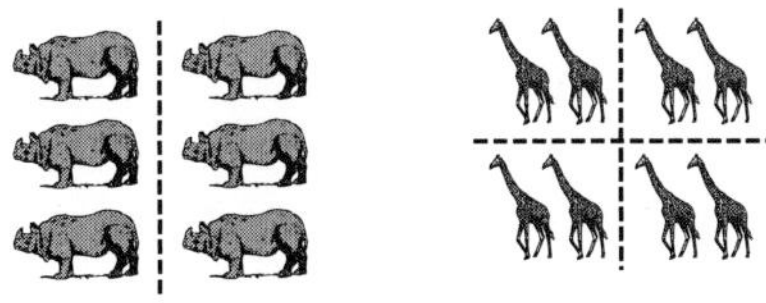

quarters halves

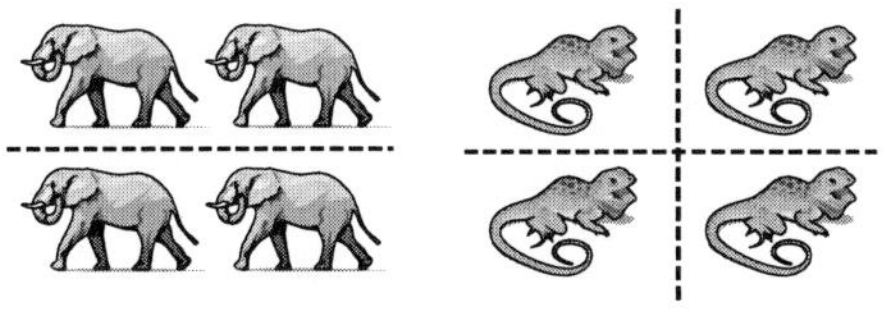

quarters halves

❸ **a** 10 : 00 ______ o'clock **b** 4 : 00 ______ o'clock

13:3

, **10 – 6 – 2 =** ☐

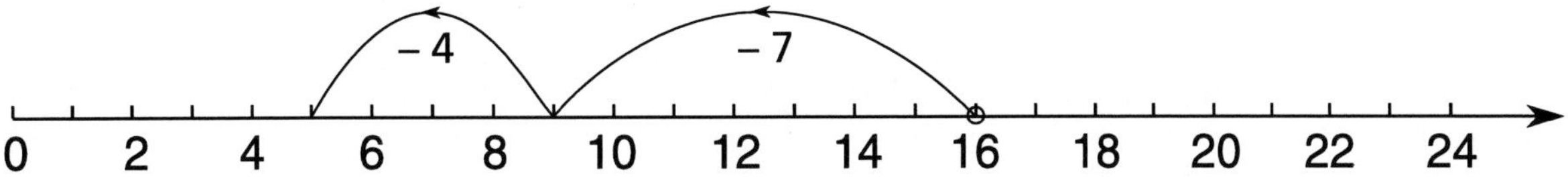

❶ We can use a number line to subtract numbers. 16 – 7 – 4 = 5

a 10 – 7 – 2 = ______

b 18 – 8 – 4 = ______

c 12 – 2 – 6 = ______

d 17 – 9 – 1 = ______

e 14 – 6 – 3 = ______

f 24 – 5 – 7 = ______

☐ groups of five owls = ☐

❶

8	7	6	8
+ 6	+ 9	+ 8	+ 7
____	____	____	____

❷

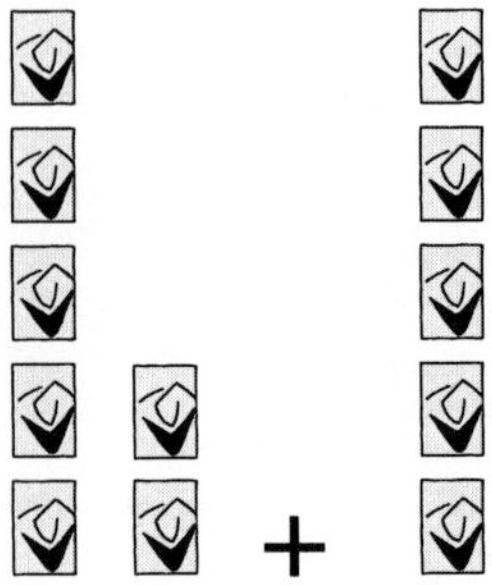

7 + 5 = ______

12 − 5 = ______

12 − 7 = ______

❸ Draw a kite.

How many sides? ______

How many corners? ______

❹

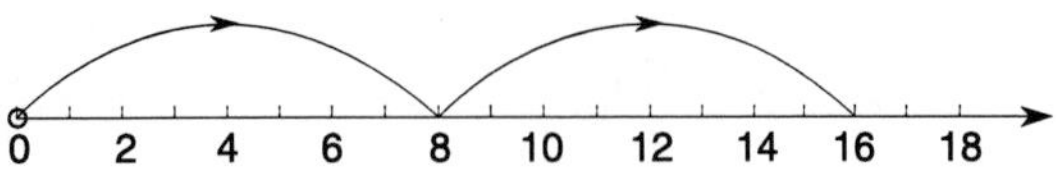

Complete:

______ + ______ = ______

❺ Possible or impossible?
You will find $5 tomorrow.

____

❻ Draw two trapeziums.

❼ Copy this object.

❽ Colour one quarter of this group.

❾ 19 − 7 = ______

12 − 2 = ______

❿

41	42	43	44	45	46	47	48	49	50
51	52	53	54	55	56	57	58	59	60
61	62	63	64	65	66	67	68	69	70
71	72	73	74	75	76	77	78	79	80
81	82	83	84	85	86	87	88	89	90
91	92	93	94	95	96	97	98	99	100

a Count backwards by tens starting from 100. Colour these red.

b Count backwards by fives starting from 100.
Circle these as you go.

c Count by twos starting from 42.
Shade these as you go.

14:2

 , ☐ groups of ☐ = ☐

❶ Circle the fair shares.

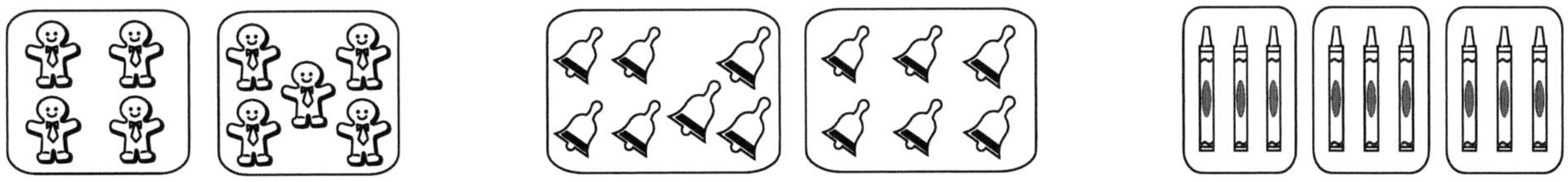

❷ What fraction of each shape is coloured?

__________ __________ __________ __________

❸ Draw a ball on the **right** of the fence.
Draw a cat on the **left** of the fence.

14:3

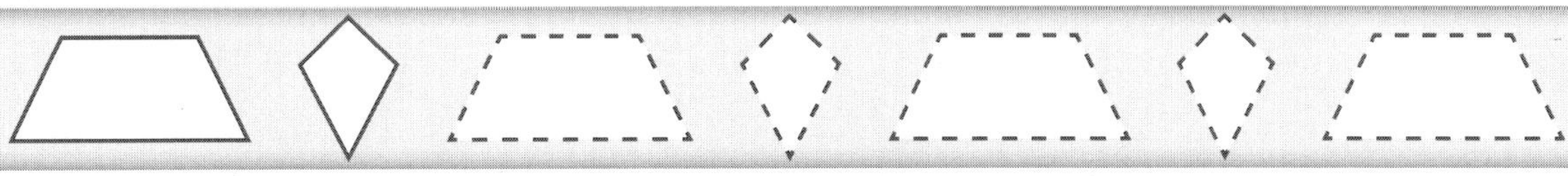

❶ Write a number sentence to match each number line.

a

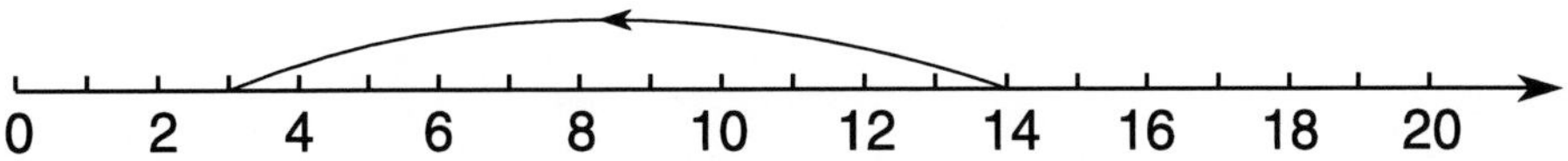

☐ − ☐ = ☐

b

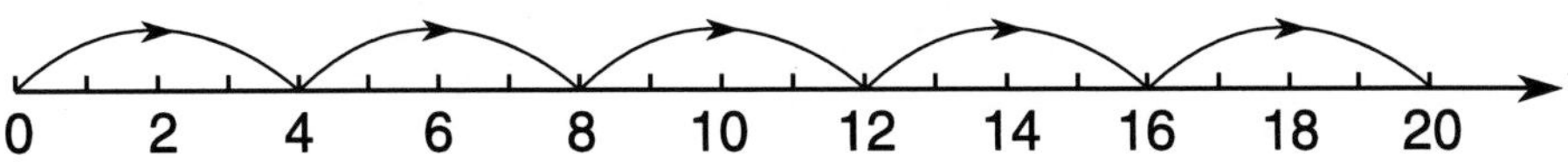

☐ × ☐ = ☐

❷ Make up your own number sentences. Show them on the number line.

a

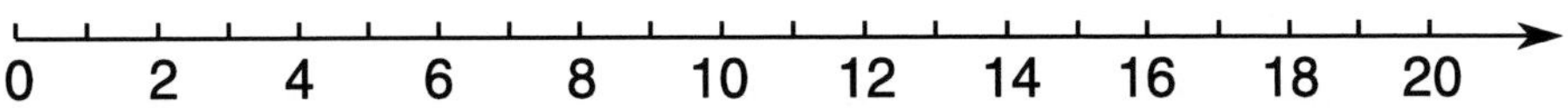

☐

b

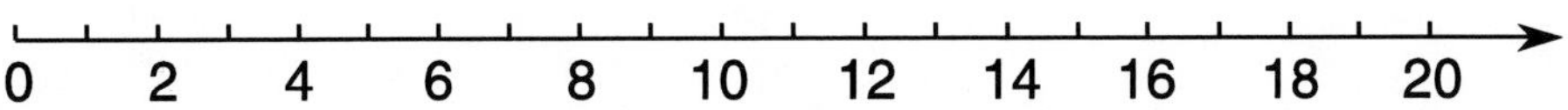

☐

☐ groups of ☐ balls = ☐

15:1

, ☐ × ☐ = ☐

1

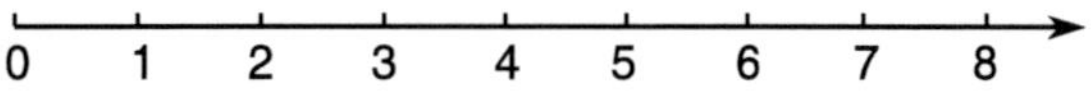

5 + 3 = ____   3 + 5 = ____

8 – 3 = ____   8 – 5 = ____

2

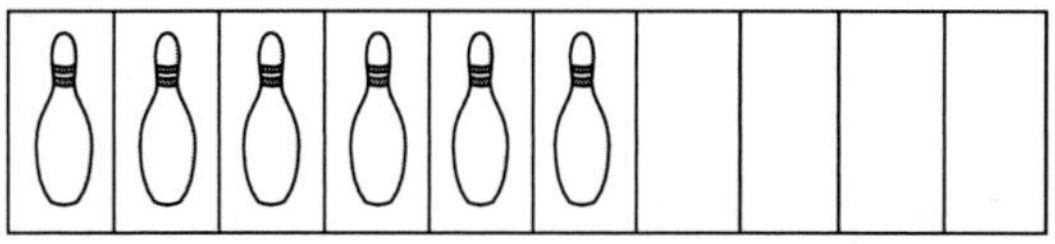

6 + ______ = 10

10 – 6 = ______

10 – 4 = ______

3 Draw 2 parallel lines on the left side of this rhombus.

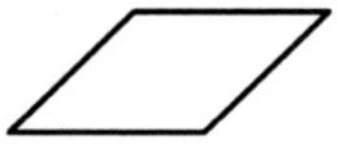

4 Share 6 lollies between 2 children.

6 ÷ 2 = ______

5 Draw a bird on the left of the tree and a cat to the right.

6 Circle groups of five.

How many groups of 5? ____

How many altogether? ____

7 Write the time in words.

9 : 15

____

8 How many tens in 60? ____

9 Complete each number web.

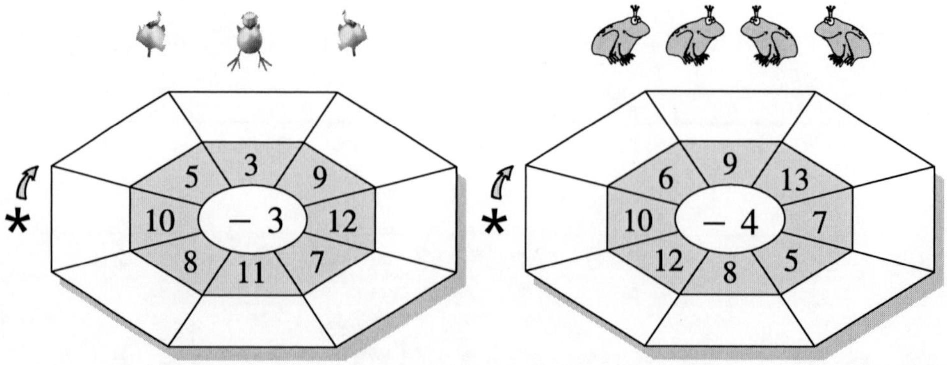

 • *AUSTRALIAN SIGNPOST MATHS 2 MENTALS* • ISBN 978 1 4886 2180 2

15:2

❶ Match these shapes with the names.

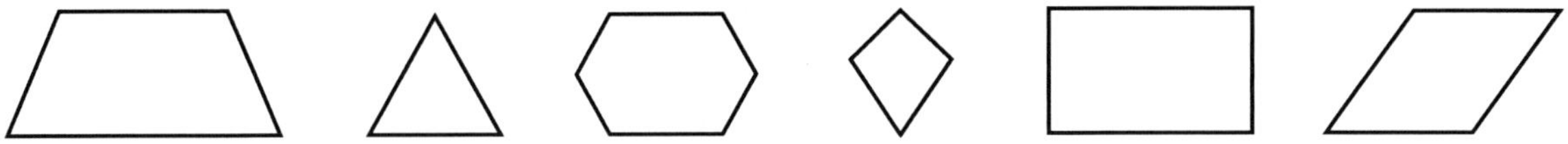

triangle trapezium rectangle kite hexagon rhombus

❷ **a** How many birds? ______

b How many more dogs than cats? ______

c How many animals altogether? ______

Animals in the Park

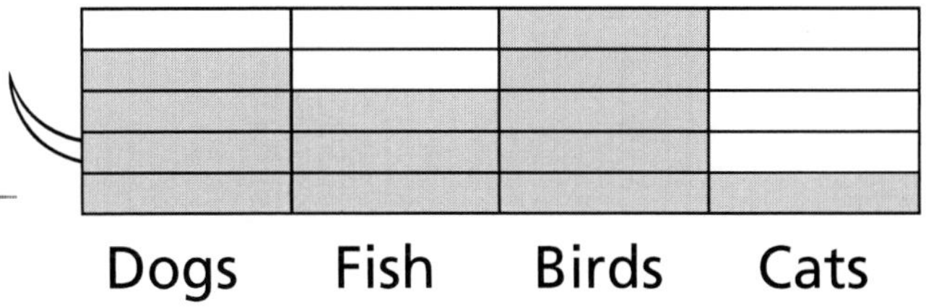

15:3

5 : 45 **That's 'quarter to 6' or 'forty-five minutes past five'.**

❶ Write two ways we can say the time shown.

a

b

c

16:1

, ☐ × ☐ = ☐

❶ 8 + 4 = ____ 6 + 7 = ____

❷ 

3 + ______ = 10

10 – 3 = ______

10 – 7 = ______

❸ Each bundle has 10 tens. What number is modelled here? ________

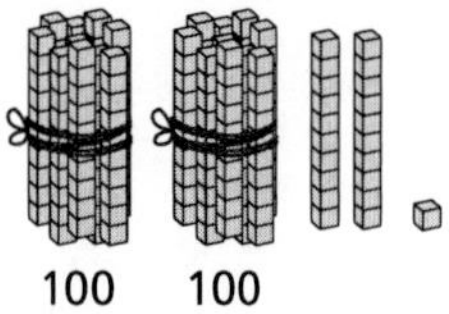

❹ Draw a pair of parallel lines in this box.

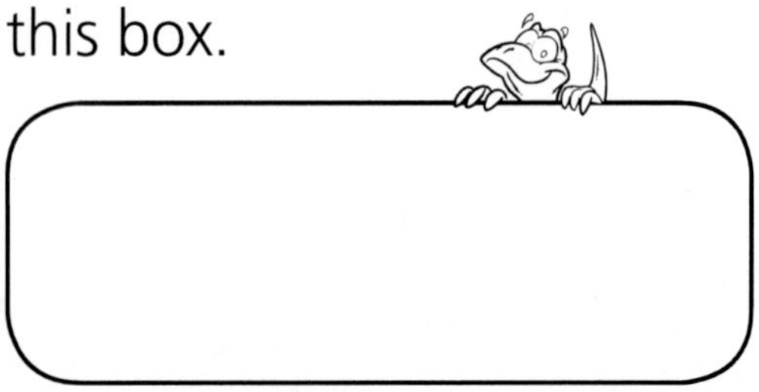

❺ 

How many groups of 3 bears? ______

❻ Which is heavier, a worm or a fish? ____________

❼ Write the time in words.

7 : 45

____

❽ Colour the shorter snake.

❾ Complete each number web.

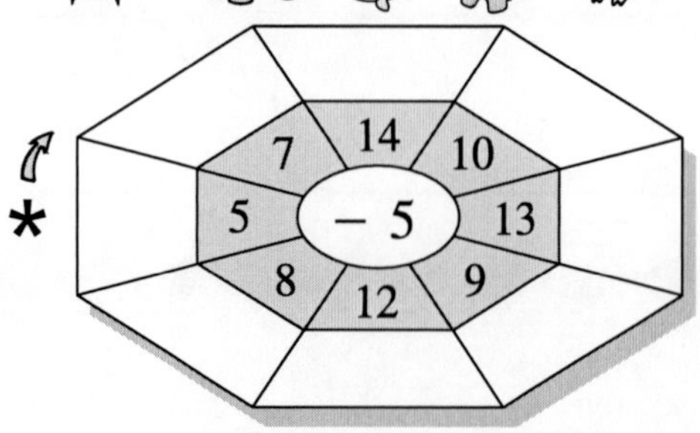

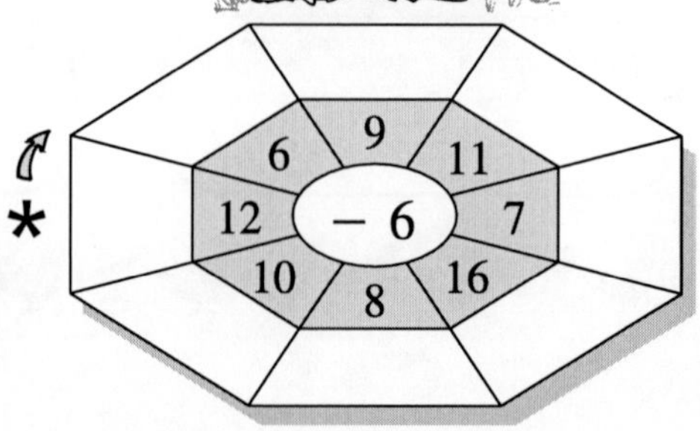

 ISBN 978 1 4886 2180 2

16:2

☐ ice creams

❶ Ten ice creams are shared among 5 children.

One fair share = ______________________

❷ Ros tossed a coin 30 times and recorded the results below.

Use these results to complete the graph.

H	T	H	T	T	H	T	H	H	T	H	H	T	H	H
H	H	H	T	H	T	H	H	T	T	H	T	T	T	T

a Colour one box for each toss of the coin.

Heads																				
Tails																				

b Which was tossed more often, heads or tails? ______

16:3

☐ plums

❶ Write each number shown.

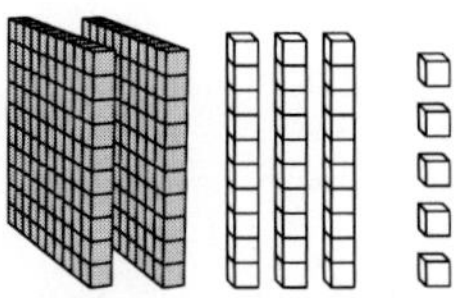

200 | 30 | 5

= 235

a 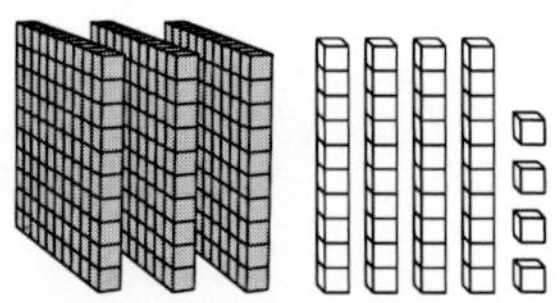 ______

b 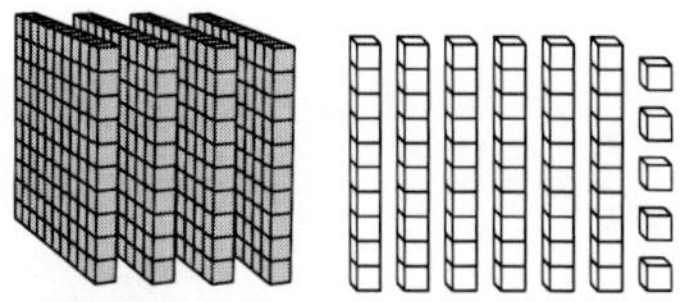 ______

c  ______

d 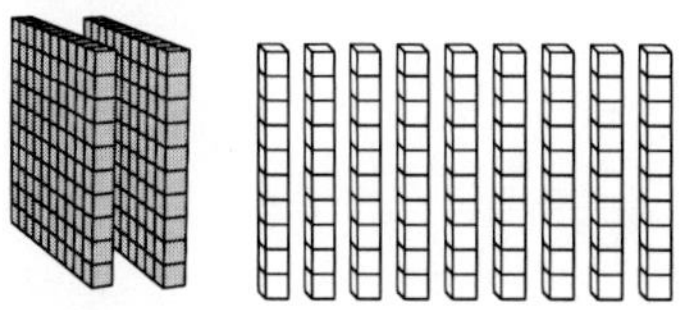 ______

e 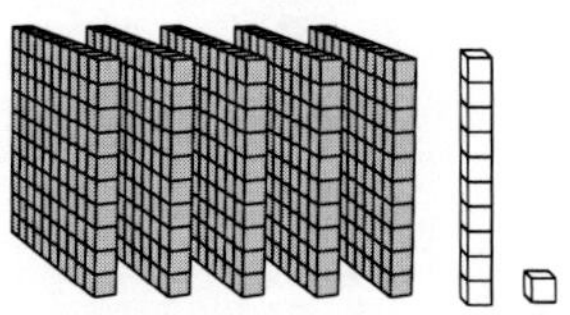 ______

f 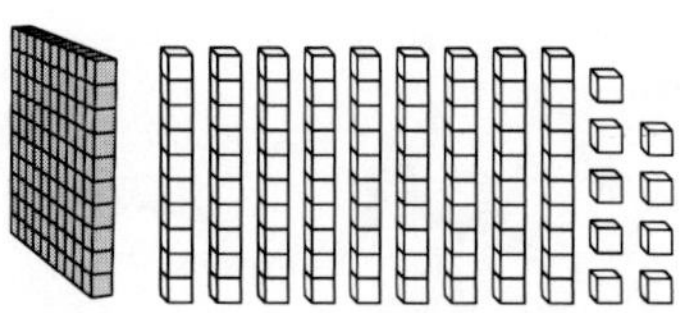 ______

How many kangaroos? ☐

 • *AUSTRALIAN SIGNPOST MATHS 2 MENTALS* • ISBN 978 1 4886 2180 2

17:1

, ☐ **groups of** ☐ = ☐

1

a 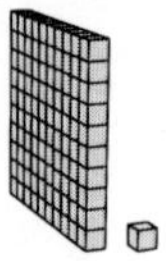 ______

b 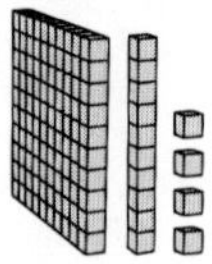 ______

2 a 4 + 7 + 6 + 3 = ______

b 9 + 3 + 7 + 1 + 2 = ______

3 Circle the largest number and write the numbers in order.

44 97 135 70

____

4 Colour half of each shape.

5 Write the numerals for:

thirteen ______

nineteen ______

6 Colour one quarter of each.

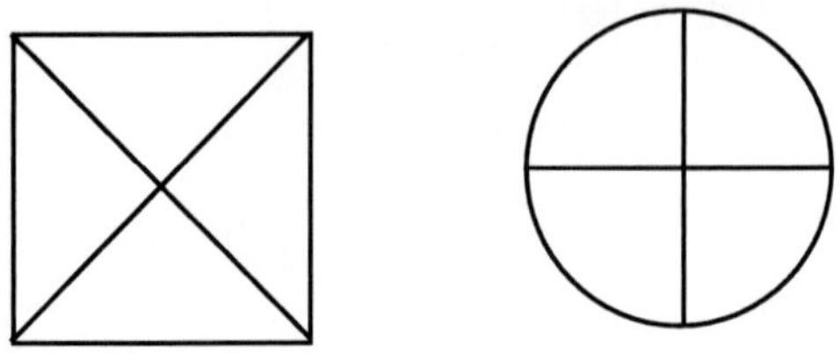

7 Circle the straight line.

8 Colour $\frac{1}{4}$ of the balls.

9 What day is it today?

____

10 What fraction is coloured?

______

11

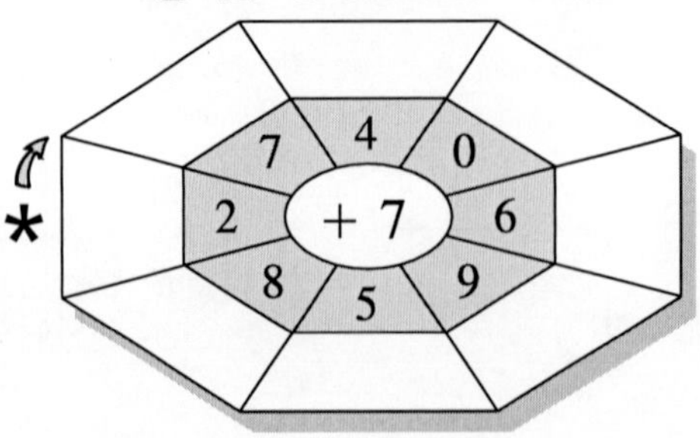

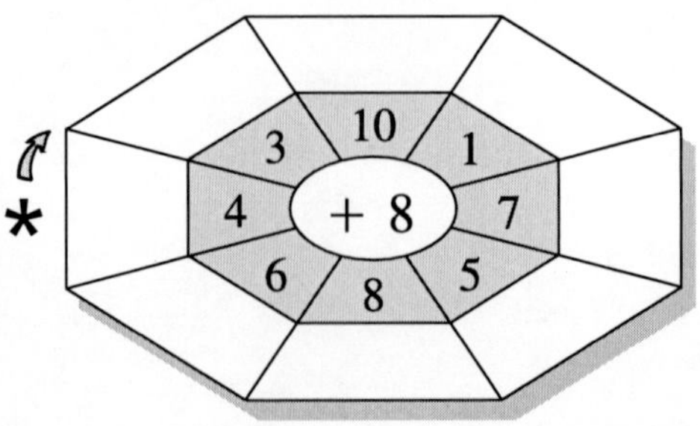

 ISBN 978 1 4886 2180 2

Answers

Answers ID Card A

1 addition **2** subtraction **3** multiplication **4** division **5** is equal to **6** number line **7** ordinal numbers **8** ones (place-value) block **9** tens (place-value) block **10** hundreds (place-value) block **11** half **12** quarter **13** eighth **14** dollar sign **15** gold coins: $1, $2 **16** silver coins: 50c, 20c, 10c, 5c **17** $5 notes **18** $10 notes **19** $20 notes **20** $50 notes **21** $100 notes **22** 3 o'clock **23** half past 9 **24** quarter past 4 **25** quarter to 8 **26** digital time (3 o'clock) **27** hand span **28** equal arm balance **29** left hand **30** right hand

Answers ID Card B

1 circle **2** oval **3** triangle **4** square **5** rectangle **6** rhombus **7** trapezium **8** parallelogram **9** pentagon **10** hexagon **11** flip **12** slide **13** turn **14** sphere **15** cube **16** cylinder **17** cone **18** pyramid **19** prism **20** corner **21** edge **22** face **23** flat surface **24** curved surface **25** straight line **26** curved line **27** zigzag line **28** broken line **29** parallel lines **30** tally

1.1

10 + 2 = 12

❶ 3, 8

❷ **a** △, ○ **b** ▭, □

❸ 2 o'clock ❹ 2 ❺ 17

❻ two, four, seven, eleven, twenty

❼ 5c 10c 20c 50c

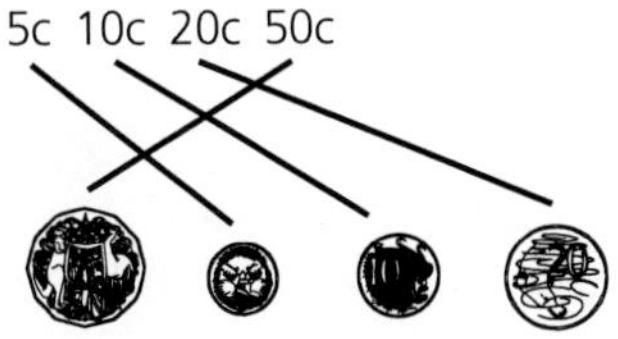

❽ 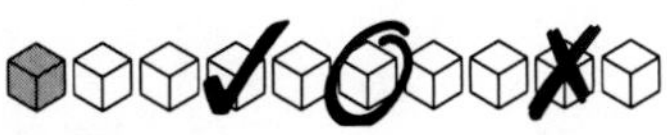

❾

21	22	23	(24)	25	26	(27)	28	(29)	30
31	32	(33)	(34)	(35)	36	37	38	(39)	(40)
41	(42)	43	(44)	45	(46)	47	(48)	49	(50)

1.2

10 suns

❶ **a** 8 **b** 7 **c** 8
d 10 **e** 10 **f** 6

❷ **a** half past eight or eight thirty, 8:30
b half past twelve or twelve thirty, 12:30
c half past five or five thirty, 5:30

❸ 37, 50, 64, 73, 96

1.3

14 balls

❶ **a** 61, 62, 63, 64, 65, 66, 67, 68, 69
b 87, 88, 89, 90, 91, 92, 93, 94, 95
c **48**, 49, 50, 51, 52, 53, 54, 55, 56
d 30, 29, 28, 27, 26, 25, 24, 23, 22

3 bananas, 11 apples, 5 cupcakes

2.1

❶ 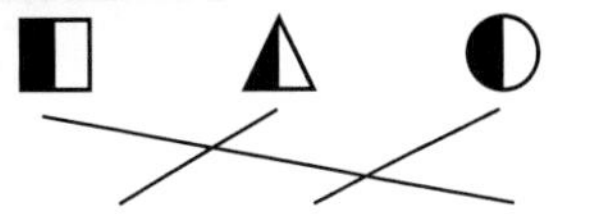

triangle circle square

❷ 4 ❸ 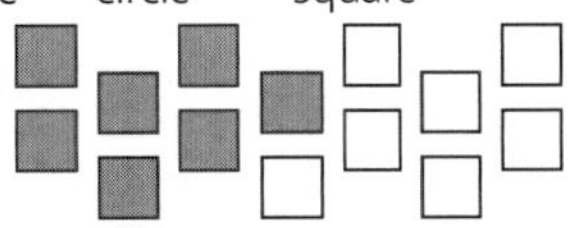

❹ 4, 4, 1, 2 ❺ 4, 6

❻ 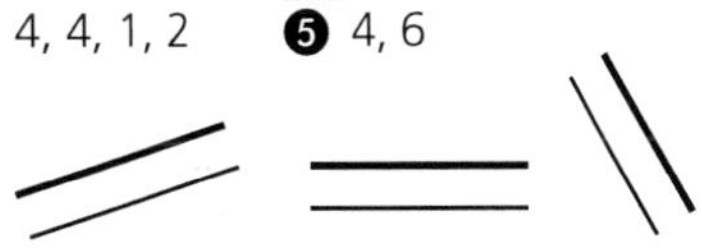

❼ 8 ❽ 5, 10 ❾ 7, 6, 9, 9

❿ **a** forty, 40 **b** seventy, 70
c fifty, 50 **d** sixty, 60

2.2

10 boats

❶ **a** 8 **b** 6 **c** 3
d 5 **e** 7 **f** 0

❷ 10, 6, 8, 8

Half of each group will be coloured.

❸ 6 o'clock, 11 o'clock, 3 o'clock

2.3

❶ Your teacher may test you.

10 sheep, 10 lizards

3.1

7 bones

❶ 8 − 3 = 5 ❷ 

 AUSTRALIAN SIGNPOST MATHS 2 MENTALS • ISBN 978 1 4886 2180 2

❸ 

❹ 

❺ 8, 7, 10 ❻ Jim

❼ A pair of parallel lines will be drawn.

❽ half past 1, half past 8

❾ 4, 9, 6, 5, 8, 3, 10, 7
7, 9, 3, 6, 11, 10, 8, 5

3.2

5 + 5 = 10

❶ a ■■□□ b ●●●○○○
c ▲▼▲▽△▽

❷ 7, 10, 9, 9, 7

❸ triangle, rhombus, rectangle

❹ 

3.3

5 + 4 = 9

❶ Estimates will vary. ❷ 10 (cartons)
 79 butterflies.

4.1

8

❶ 40, 45, 50, 55, 60

❷ 4, 4, 4. A quarter of each shape will be shaded.

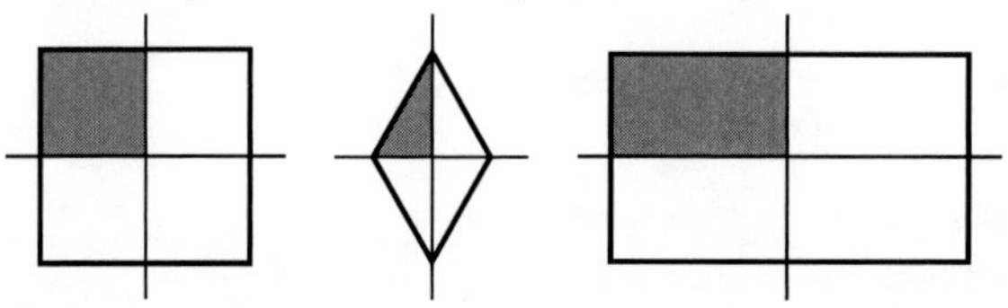

❸ 6, 3

❹ 

❺ 2, 4, 6, 8, 10, 12, 14

❻ $1, 5c, 50c, $2

❼ 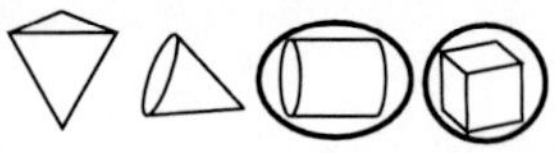

❽ C

❾ a  b  c 

4.2

❶ 68, 50, 61

❷ 6:00, 3:30, 4:30, 9:30

4.3

65, 70, 75

❶ a 100, 98, 96, 94, 92, 90, 88
b 100, 90, 80, 70, 60, 50, 40
c 100, 95, 90, 85, 80, 75, 70
d 79, 77, 75, 73, 71, 69, 67, 65, 63
e 89, 79, 69, 59, 49, 39, 29, 19, 9

 8 groups of ten dogs = 80

5.1

8 − 2 = 6

❶ 5, 3 ❷ 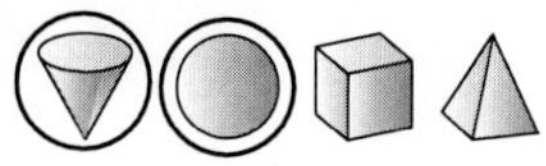

❸ Answers will vary, for example, apple.

❹ Answers will vary.

❺ 11, 14

❻ 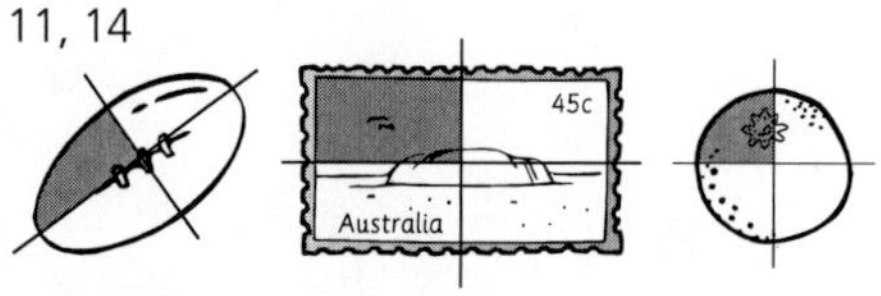

❼ 5, 8, 10, 10

❽ 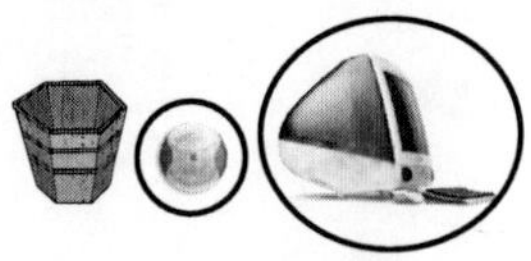

❾ 

❿ a 2 tens b 3 tens c 20 tens

5.2

10 + 2 = 12

❶ a 120 b 132 c 128

❷ a 116 b 129 c 102

❸ a 73, 75, 77, 79, 81
b 79, 89, 99, 109, 119
c 82, 87, 92, 97, 102
d 93, 103, 113, 123, 133

❹ 3

5.3

7 + 3 = 10

1. **a** 10 **b** 13 **c** 17 **d** 15 **e** 20
   f 19 **g** 24 **h** 29 **i** 28

 75 stars

6.1

8 − 5 = 3

1. 5 tens 4 ones = 54
2. triangle, 3, 3
3. 12, 12, 11, 13
4. 5 Tens = 50
5. Answers will vary.
   One answer could be 10 + 3 = 13 and 2 + 4 + 2 = 8.
6. 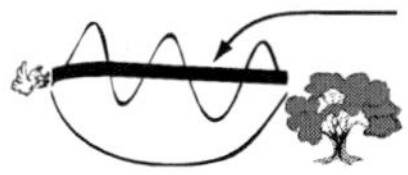 This is the shortest path.
7. 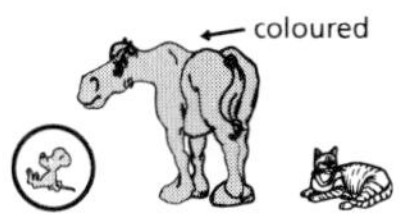

8. 36, 37, 38, 39, 40
9. 0, 2, 4, 5, 6, 7, 8, 9
   4, 7, 3, 6, 5, 1, 8, 0

6.2

1. 14, 14, 17, 17, 13
2. **a** 5 paperclips **b** 7 paperclips

6.3

1. **a** 2, 4, 6, 8, 10, 12, 14, 16
   b 22, 24, 26, 28, 30, 32, 34
   c 5, 10, 15, 20, 25, 30, 35
   d 10, 20, 30, 40, 50, 60, 70
   e 100, 110, 120, 130, 140, 150

● 10 groups of ten dots = 100

7.1

35, 40, 45

1. 10, 10, 11, 9
2. 3 rows of 7 = 21
3. 6:15 or a quarter past 6

4. 
5. 4 tens, 8 ones = 48
6. 10, 20
7. Answers will vary.
8. 40, 60
9. 8:45 or a quarter to 9
10. **a** 19, 4 **b** 34, 9

7.2

6

1. 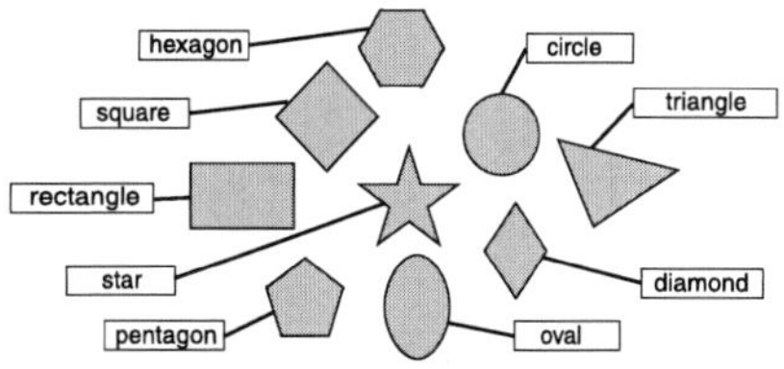

2. **a** 36, 37, 38, 39, 40
   b 22, 21, 20, 19, 18
   c 10, 20, 30, 40, 50
   d 2, 4, 6, 8, 10

7.3

18

1. **a** 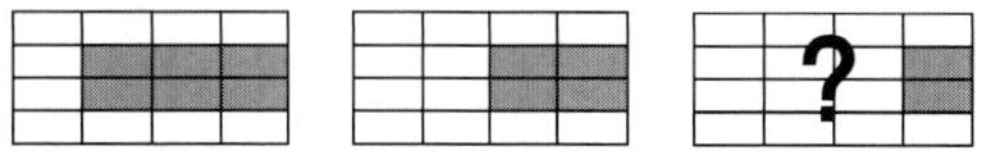

   6 grey tiles, 10 white tiles; 4 grey tiles, 12 white tiles; 2 grey tiles, 14 white tiles
   b 20 grey tiles
   c 44 white tiles

 62 elephants

8.1

1 o'clock, 4 o'clock

1. 16, 16, 15, 17
2.  3 groups of 8 = 24
3. 12 + 6 = 18
4. **a** 89 **b** 51
5. 10:15 or a quarter past 10
6. 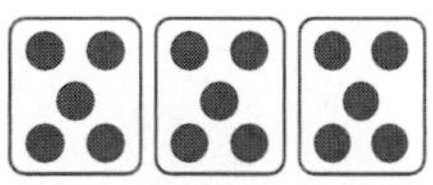 Each girl is given 5 counters.
7. 18, 14
8. 2 rows of 10 = 20
9. 0, 3, 4, 5, 6, 7, 8, 9
   4, 7, 1, 0, 8, 3, 6, 2

8.2

1. 3 rows of 6 = 18
2. 4 groups of 9 = 36
3. **a** 8 **b** 11 **c** 4 **d** 41

8.3

1. Half of each shape will be coloured.

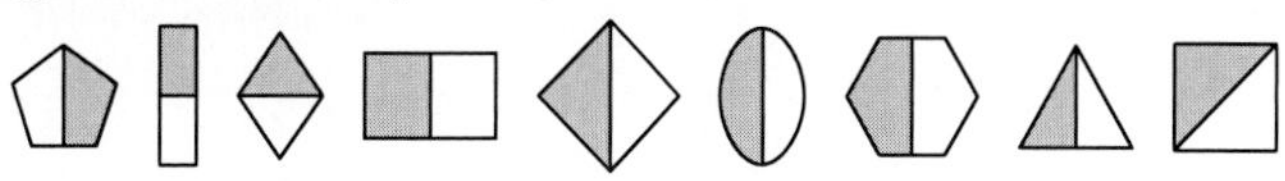

 78 tops

9.1

2 groups of 4 = 8

❶ 30, 50 ❷ 10, 9

❸ 17
−5
12 (cars)

❹ There will be 3 lollies in each group.
3 each

❺ 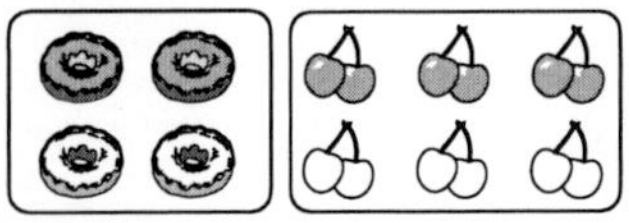
Half of each is coloured.

❻ 5 groups of 2 = 10, 5 × 2 = 10

❼ 3, 15, 9

❽ 

❾ a  b 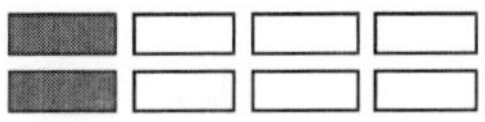

❿ Answers will vary.
One answer could be 10 + 3 + 1 = 14.

⓫ 5, 10, 7, 3, 9, 12, 8, 11
8, 7, 13, 14, 11, 9, 12, 10

9.2

❶ a 34 b 4 c 2 d 56

❷ 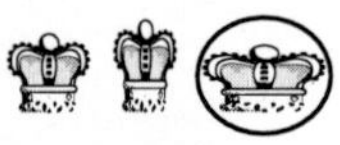

❸ 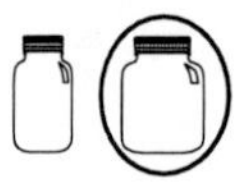

9.3

❶ 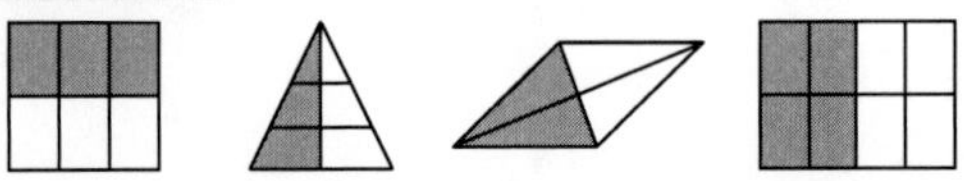

Answers will vary. Half of each shape will be coloured.

❷ 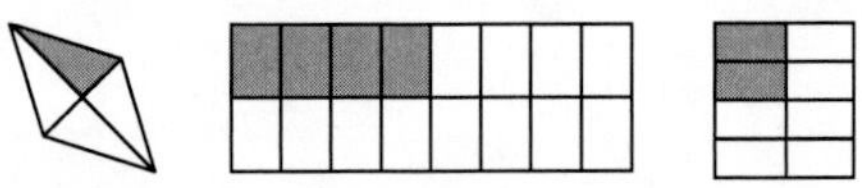

Answers will vary. A quarter of each shape will be coloured.

12 groups of 5 balls = 60

10.1

7 − 3 = 4

❶ 8 tens, 80

❷ a 422 b 297 c 840 d 568

❸ 3, 4 ❹ yes

❺ 19
−5
14 (cakes)

❻ Answers will vary.
One answer could be 10 + 4 + 3 = 17.

❼ 

❽ 577 ❾ pentagon, 5, 5 ❿ 7, 10

⓫ 10, 11, 12, 13, 14, 15, 16, 17
15, 19, 12, 13, 17, 14, 18, 20

10.2

10th

❶ One face on each shape will be shaded.

❷ 

❸ 9, 8, 9, 9, 11

10.3

❶ a 9 b 12 c 8
d 16 e 21 f 24

 8 groups of eight cows = 64

11.1

4 × 2 = 8

❶ 4 rows of 5 = 20, 4 × 5 = 20

❷ Half of the ladybugs will be circled.

❸ 13
−4
9 (stars)

❹ 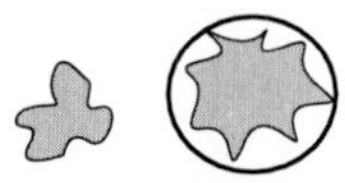

❺ 6, 5 ❻ 3, 4, 4 ❼ unlikely

❽ 9 tens = 90

❾ 34, 35, 36, 37, 38, 39

❿ 7 tens 0 ones

⓫ a 310 b 420 c 504
d 847 e 721

11.2

3 groups of 3 = 9

❶ 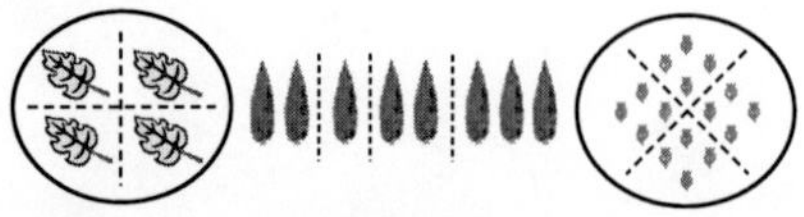

❷ 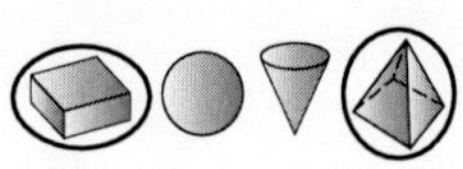

 ISBN 978 1 4886 2180 2

❸ There will be 5 balls drawn in each box.
3 groups of 5 = 15, 3 × 5 = 15

11.3

❶ a 10, 20, 30, 40, 50, 60, 70
Rule: Add 10.
b 4, 14, 24, 34, 44, 54, 64
Rule: Add 10.
c 7, 17, 27, 37, 47, 57, 67
Rule: Add 10.
d 21, 31, 41, 51, 61, 71, 81
Rule: Add 10.

 10 lollies,  13 birds,  16 butterflies

12.1

❶ 14, 13

❷  1 (corner), 1 (edge), 2 (surfaces)

❸  3 groups of 2 flowers will be drawn
3 groups of 2 = 6
3 × 2 = 6

❹ cylinder ❺ 459 ❻ 4 + 4 = 8, 8

❼ Answers will vary. Students will write an event that has no chance of happening.

❽ 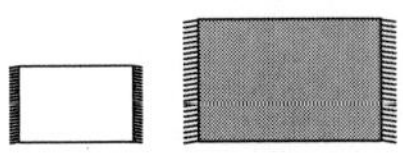

❾ 13, 17

❿ 9, 8, 7, 6, 5, 4, 3, 2
5, 1, 10, 7, 3, 6, 2, 0

12.2

10 − 4 = 6

❶ 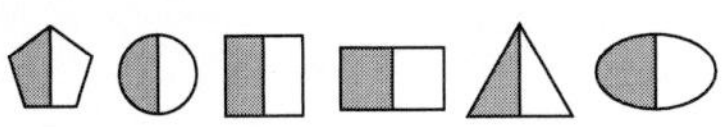

❷ a 3 b 7 c 9

❸ 

The first car is coloured red.

12.3

13

❶ a 13 b 22 c 20 d 23
e 22 f 23

 63 seals

13.1

6 + 7 = 13

❶ 9 ❷ 3, 8

❸ 2 counters will be drawn in each box.

❹ 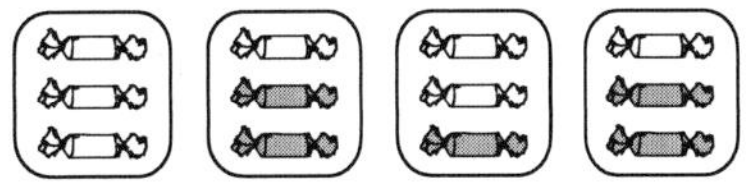

4 groups of 3 = 12

❺ number line

❻ a 6 b 10 c 60

❼  0 (corners)
2 (edges)
3 (surfaces)

❽ 2 rows of 8 = 16, 2 × 8 = 16

❾ 7, 12, 9, 5, 11, 14, 10, 13
10, 9, 15, 16, 13, 11, 14, 12

13.2

3 groups of 3 = 9

❶ 8 (dogs)

❷ 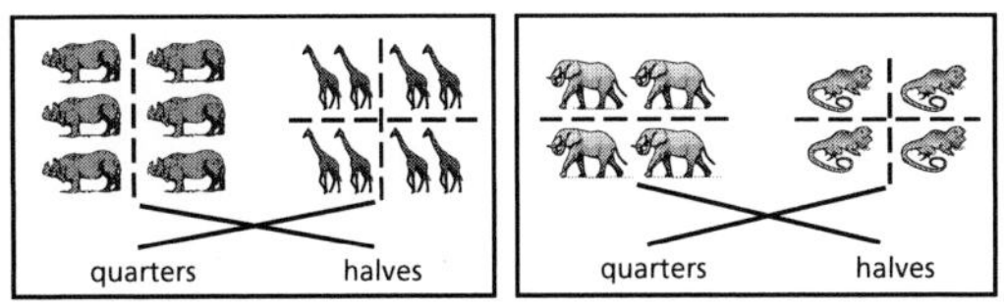

❸ a 10 (o'clock) b 4 (o'clock)

13.3

10 − 6 − 2 = 2

❶ a 1 b 6 c 4 d 7
e 5 f 12

 10 groups of five owls = 50

14.1

❶ 14, 16, 14, 15 ❷ 12, 7, 5

❸ 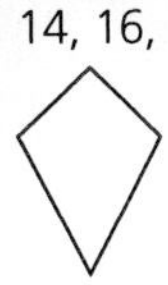 4, 4

❹ 8 + 8 = 16 ❺ possible

❻ 2 trapeziums will be drawn.

❼ 

❽ 

❾ 12, 10

 • *AUSTRALIAN SIGNPOST MATHS 2 MENTALS* • ISBN 978 1 4886 2180 2

10

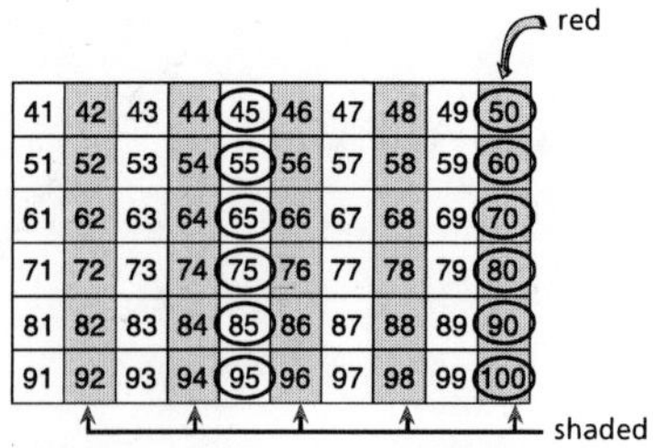

14.2

4 groups of 3 = 12

1 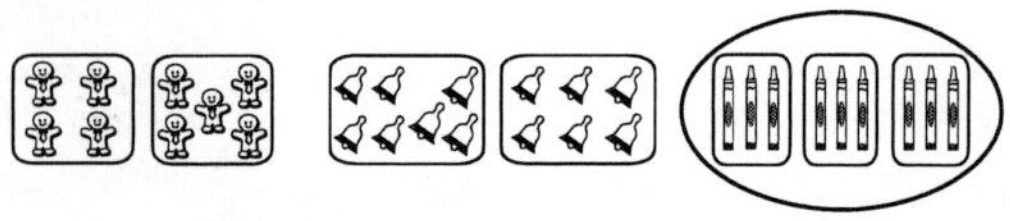

2 one quarter or $\frac{1}{4}$, one half or $\frac{1}{2}$,
one half or $\frac{1}{2}$, one quarter or $\frac{1}{4}$

3 

14.3

1 a 14 – 11 = 3   b 5 × 4 = 20

2 a–b Answers will vary.

18 groups of 2 balls = 36

15.1

3 × 4 = 12

1 8, 8, 5, 3 2 4, 4, 6 3 

4 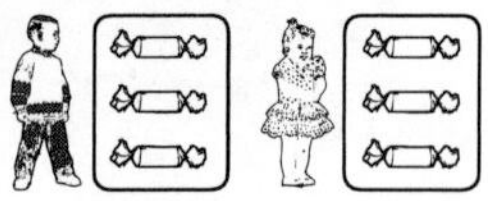

5 

6  5 groups of 5, 25 altogether

7 a quarter past nine or nine fifteen

8 6

9 7, 2, 0, 6, 9, 4, 8, 5
6, 2, 5, 9, 3, 1, 4, 8

15.2

1 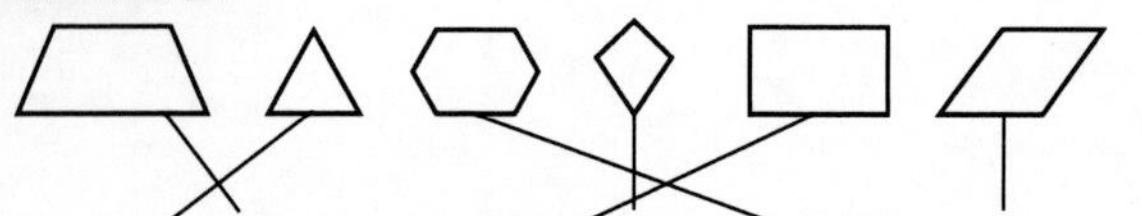

2 a 5   b 3   c 13

15.3

1 a two fifteen, a quarter past 2
b eleven forty-five or a quarter to 12
c five fifteen or a quarter past 5

 16 camels,  18 hens,  18 cows

16.1

3 × 3 = 9

1 12, 13 2 7, 7, 3 3 221

4 A pair of parallel lines will be drawn. 5 6 6 a fish

7 seven forty-five, forty-five past 7 or a quarter to 8

8 The shorter snake will be coloured.

9 0, 2, 9, 5, 8, 4, 7, 3
6, 0, 3, 5, 1, 10, 2, 4

16.2

10 ice creams

1 2 ice creams

2 a 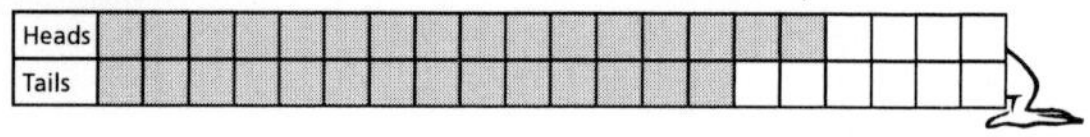

b Heads

16.3

8 plums

a 344   b 465   c 700   d 290
e 511   f 199

 68 kangaroos

17.1

3 groups of 4 = 12

1 a 101   b 114   2 a 20   b 22

3 135 will be circled; 44, 70, 97, 135

4 

5 13, 19

6 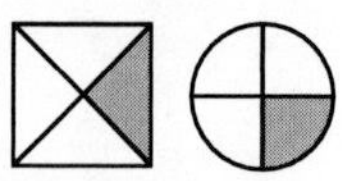

7 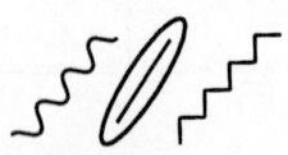

8 

9 Answers will vary.

10 one out of 4 or $\frac{1}{4}$

11 9, 14, 11, 7, 13, 16, 12, 15
12, 11, 18, 9, 15, 13, 16, 14

© PEARSON AUSTRALIA 2018 • *AUSTRALIAN SIGNPOST MATHS 2 MENTALS* • ISBN 978 1 4886 2180 2

17.2

❶ a 20 b 4 c 5 d 20
❷ a 12 b 4 c 3 d 12
❸ a 3 b 2 c 9

17.3

❶ 33, 34, 35, 36, 37, 38, 39

 80 spiders

18.1

❶ a 129 b 112
❷ 21, 23, 22, $27
❸
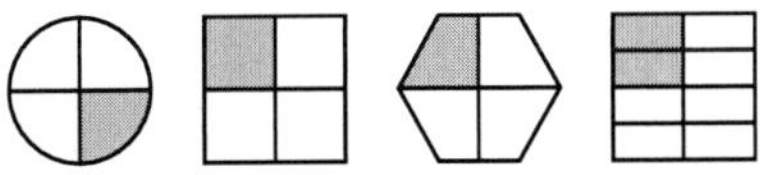

❹ 26, 36, 46, <u>56</u>, <u>66</u>, <u>76</u>
83, 73, 63, <u>53</u>, <u>43</u>, <u>33</u>
❺ thirty-five ❻ two out of 6 or $\frac{2}{6}$
❼ 152 ❽ 66, 62
❾ Answers will vary.
❿
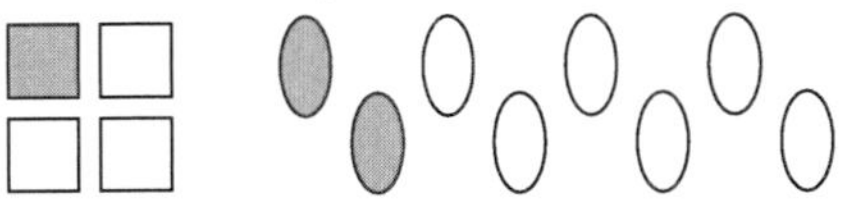

A quarter of each group will be coloured. Other answers are possible.

⓫

$\frac{1}{2}$ will be coloured.
Other answers are possible.

⓬ 12, 13, 14, 15, 16, 17, 18, 19
10, 3, 4, 5, 6, 7, 8, 9

18.2

❶ a 10 b 18 c 8
d February (There are 28 days in this month.)
❷

18.3

24

❶ a 17 b 24 c 12 d 21 e 20
f 10 g 23 h 24

 10 pelicans,  26 pumas,  12 paw prints

19.1

9 – 3 = 6

❶ 18, 28, 38, <u>48</u>, <u>58</u>, <u>68</u>
75, 65, 55, <u>45</u>, <u>35</u>, <u>25</u>

❷ 5, 5 ❸ yes (Answers may vary.)

❹ Answers will vary.
One answer could be 7 + 6 = 13.
❺ autumn ❻ 59, 71, 43, 37
❼

127	179	100	172
170	180	189	170

❽

(Answers may vary.)

❾

❿ a slide

⓫ 10, 8, 7, 3, 6, 2, 5, 4
4, 9, 5, 3, 6, 8, 10, 2

19.2

❶ May, June ❷
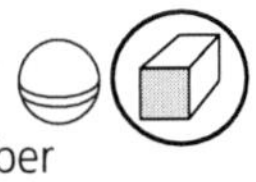

❸ February, October
❹

+	7	5	8	6	9	4
3	10	8	11	9	12	7
5	12	10	13	11	14	9

	10	7	9	5	8	6
– 5	5	2	4	0	3	1
– 3	7	4	6	2	5	3

19.3

❶ a 23 b 25 c 24 d 23
e 25 f 24 g 36 h 36

 67 sheep

20.1

❶ 4, 6 ❷ 735 ❸ greater
❹

❺ 121 will be circled.
❻

❼ 132, 355
❽ 5, 10, 15, <u>20</u>, <u>25</u>, <u>30</u>
18, 16, 14, <u>12</u>, <u>10</u>, <u>8</u>
4, 9, 14, <u>19</u>, <u>24</u>, <u>29</u>
❾ December
❿
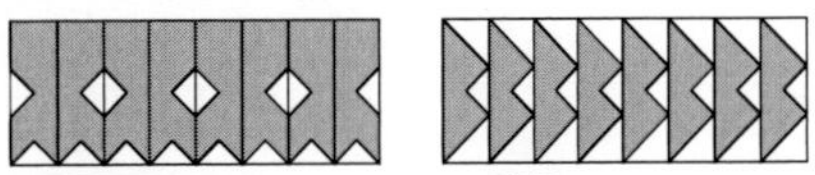

flip slide

20.2

❶ Monday; See teacher.
❷ a plum b ruler (or peg)
c 4 (pegs) d 9 (pegs)

❸ a 5, 10, 15, 20, 25, 30, 35, 40, 45, 50, 55
b 0, 10, 20, 30, 40, 50, 60, 70, 80, 90, 100

20.3

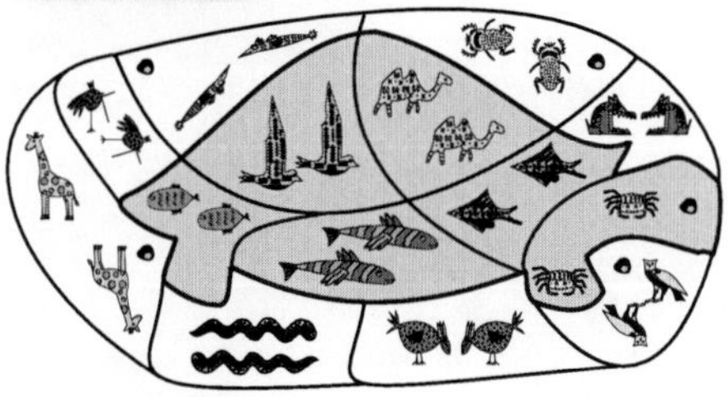

8 groups of five rabbits = 40

21.1

❶ 8, 2, 8, 2 ❷ 321 ❸ 40c

❹ 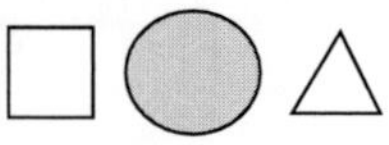

❺ 40, 45, 50, 55, 60
33, 43, 53, 63, 73

❻ January ❼ a 12 (squares)
b 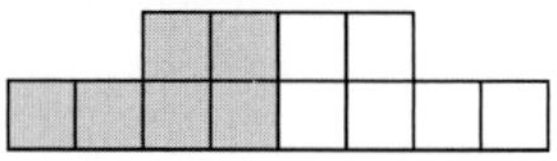

❽ 7 ❾ 17, 29

❿ 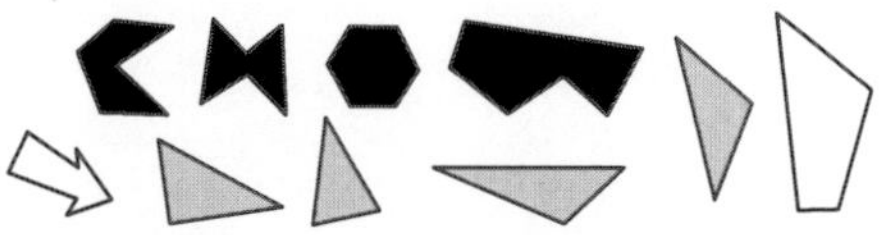

The black shapes will be coloured red. The grey shapes will be coloured blue.

21.2

2 groups of 3 = 6

❶ The 5c and 10c coins will be circled. The 50c, 5c, 10c and 20c coins will be coloured grey. The $1 coin will be coloured yellow.

❷ Answers will vary.

❸ 

21.3

20

❶ Answers will vary.
One answer could be
5 + 5 + 5 + 1 = 16 or
10 + 5 + 4 + 1 = 20

 13 groups of four ants = 52

22.1

24 cones

❶ 16, 9, 9, 9 ❷ 336, 519 ❸ 80c

❹ 16 triangles, 18 diamonds

❺ 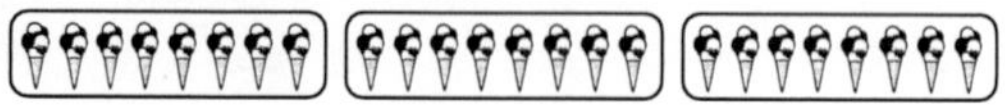
6 (groups of 4 cones)

❻ 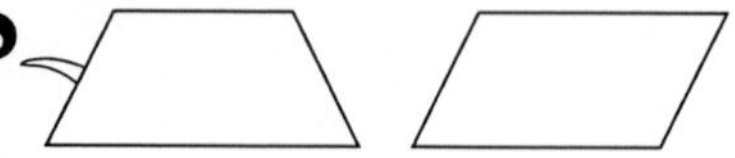

❼ 4 groups of 5 = 20, 4 × 5 = 20

❽ (5c) (5c) (5c) (5c)

❾ 9, 5, 1, 6, 8, 3, 4, 7
3, 9, 2, 0, 7, 4, 6, 10

22.2

5 × 3 = 15 blocks

❶ 

❷ 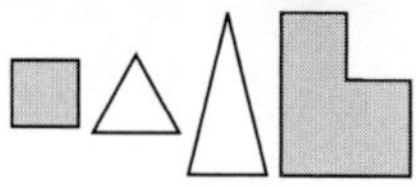

❸ 

22.3

3 × 8 = 24

❶ a 6 (bolts) b 16 (bolts) c 12 (bolts)
d 60 (bolts) e 3 (globes) f 5 (globes)

 80 camels

23.1

❶ 24 ❷ 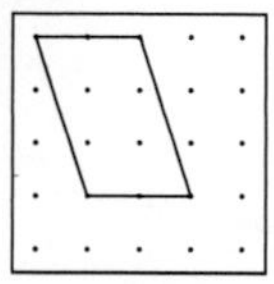 A parallelogram will be drawn.
4 (sides), 4 (corners)

❸ 8 (horns), 2 + 2 + 2 + 2 = 8

❹ A ❺ a yes b 6 ❻ 24, 33

❼ 3 + 3 = 6, 2 × 3 = 6

❽ (20c) (20c) (10c) (10c)

❾ a $10 b $15 c $12 d $11
e $7 f $4 g $8 h $9

AUSTRALIAN SIGNPOST MATHS 2 MENTALS • ISBN 978 1 4886 2180 2

23.2

❶

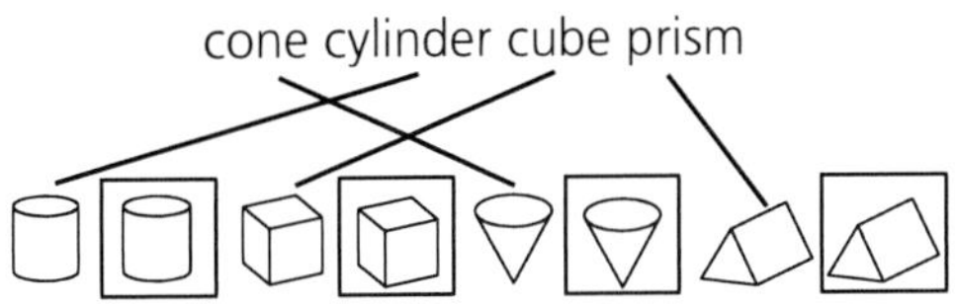

❷ 6, 14, 5, 15, 9

❸ 1st, <u>6th</u>, <u>11th</u>, <u>16th</u>, <u>21st</u>

23.3

❶ **a** 12 **b** 9 **c** 7 **d** 8
e 9 **f** 8 **g** 13 **h** 14
i 4

The pattern will have been completed.

24.1

3 × 3 = 9

❶ 4 groups of 3 = 12,
3 + 3 + 3 + 3 = 12,
4 × 3 = 12

❷ 9 ❸ 83, 23

❹ 5 groups of 2 = 10, 5 × 2 = 10

❺ $1.30 ❻ 606, 591

❼ 20 cents, 10 cents, 5 cents

❽ forty, seventy, thirty

❾ **a** 67 **b** 82 **c** 99
d 91 **e** 68 **f** 100

24.2

$1.40, $1.10, $1.05

❶ 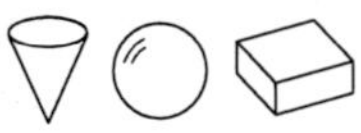

❷ Answers may vary.

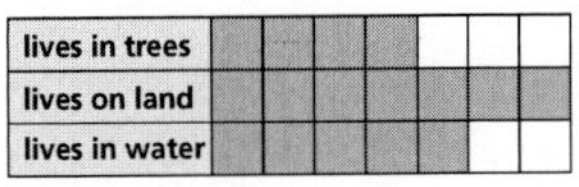

24.3

❶ **a** 2 (faces)
2 (edges)
1 (curved surface)

b 8 (faces)
18 (edges)
12 (corners)

c 1 (face)
1 (edge)
1 (curved surface)

 11 groups of five paw prints = 55

25.1

13 – 4 = 9

❶ 8 + 8 = 16, 16 ❷ 5

❸ Answers will vary. A picture will be drawn and cut in half.

❹ One quarter will be coloured.

❺ 5 ❻ 82, 42

❼ 15, 25, 35, <u>45</u>, <u>55</u>
6, 8, 10, <u>12</u>, <u>14</u>
65, 60, 55, <u>50</u>, <u>45</u>

❽ $1.80

❾ 3 groups of 8 cats = 24 cats altogether, 3 × 8 = 24

❿ **a** 4, 12, 8 **b** 12, 15, 16

25.2

❶

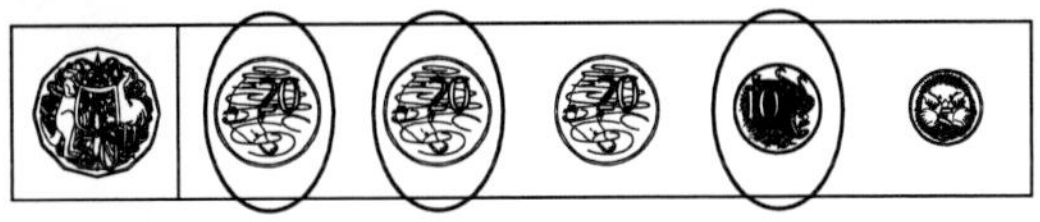

❷ **a** pink **b** yellow **c** 4 **d** 19

25.3

❶ **a** 3 globes **b** a torch
c 5 globes **d** Their mass is the same.

 36 worms

26.1

10 – 3 = 7

❶ 4 groups of 2 = 8, 4 × 2 = 8

❷ 20, 40, 80

❸

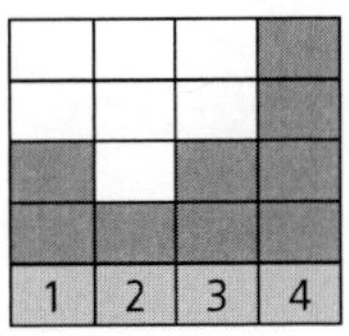

1	3
2	1
3	2
4	4

❹ 17, 13

❺ 90, 80, 70, <u>60</u>, <u>50</u>
35, 40, 45, <u>50</u>, <u>55</u>

❻ One eighth will be coloured.

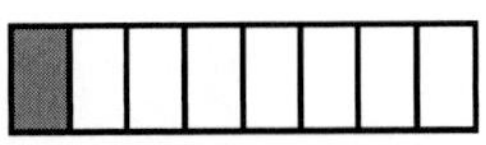

❼ 10 + 10 = 20, 20

❽ 7 tens 7 ones ❾ 9

❿ **a** 432, four hundred and thirty-two
b 294, two hundred and ninety-four
c 705, seven hundred and five

26.2

28 eagles

❶ a 50c b 55c c 35c
d 45c e 80c f 90c

❷ a F b B

26.3

❶ a quarter past 12, 12 : 15
b quarter past 11, 11 : 15
c quarter past 3, 3 : 15

 11 groups of three lizards = 33

27.1

3 × 3 = 9

❶ 6, 18, 18 ❷ 100, 60 ❸ 38, 38

❹ Answers will vary.

❺ One half will be coloured.

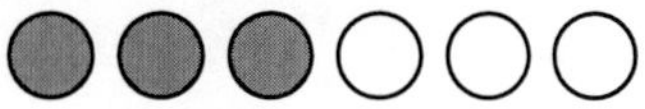

❻ 7 + 7 = 14, 14

❼ Graph: Table:

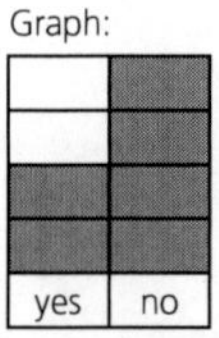

yes	2
no	4

❽ 41, 71

❾

91	92	93	94	95	96	97	98	99	100
101	102	103	104	105	106	107	108	109	110
111	112	113	114	115	116	117	118	119	120
121	122	123	124	125	126	127	128	129	130
131	132	133	134	135	136	137	138	139	140

27.2

6, 8, 7

❶ 10, 2 × 5 = 10 ❷ 12, 3 × 4 = 12

❸ spring: September, October, November
summer: December, January, February
autumn: March, April, May
winter: June, July, August

27.3

❶

 17 mice,  16 lobsters,  12 ostriches

28.1

4 × 2 = 8

❶ 3 groups of 2 = 6, 3 × 2 = 6

❷ 70 cents ❸ prism ❹ summer

❺ 87, 98, 27, 43 ❻ yes

❼ 5 tens 0 ones

❽

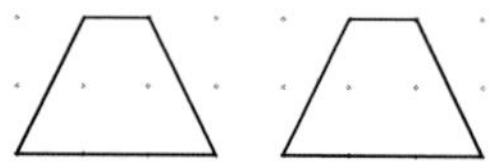

❾ spring ❿ likely (Answers may vary.)

⓫ a trapezium b triangle
c circle d square
e hexagon f oval
g rhombus h rectangle

28.2

3 x 2 = 6

❶

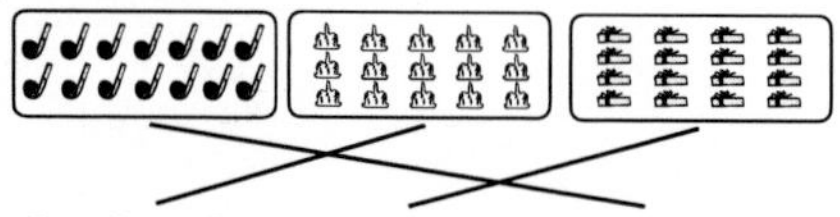

❷ 75, 85, 97

❸

28.3

10 + 10 = 20

❶ 15c, 20c, 35c, 40c, 60c, 80c, 30c, 45c

 9 antelope,  11 bats,  20 aardvarks

29.1

127, 128, 129, 130, 131, 132, 133

❶

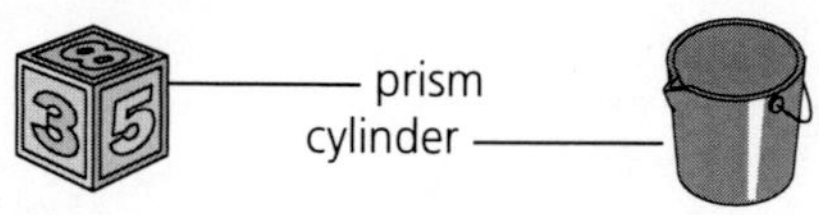

❷ likely

❸

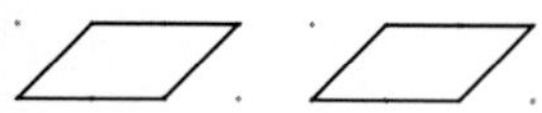

❹ Answers will vary.

❺

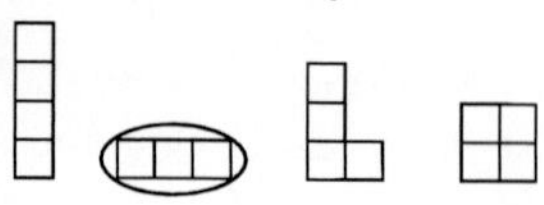

❻ 56, 74 ❼ Answers will vary.

❽ 4 (cakes) ❾ 4 (boys), 6 (boys)

❿ a January, February, March, April, May, June, July, August, September, October, November, December

b 12 c 24 d 30 e 31
f 30 g August h November

 • *AUSTRALIAN SIGNPOST MATHS 2 MENTALS* • ISBN 978 1 4886 2180 2

29.2

1. hexagon, parallelogram, rhombus, trapezium
2. 7, Thursday
3. 19th, 24th, 22nd, 30th
4. an hour

29.3

1. 15 cents (10c) (5c) — 35 cents (20c) (10c) (5c)
   25 cents (20c) (5c) — 45 cents (20c) (20c) (5c)
   30 cents (20c) (10c) — 60 cents (20c) (20c) (20c)
   40 cents (20c) (20c) — 70 cents (20c) (20c) (20c) (10c)

(Other answers are possible.)

11 reindeer, 40 crabs, 16 birds

30.1

5 × 3 = 15

1. Fishing.
2. 1, 2, 3, 4, 5, 6
3.  2 groups of 3 = 6
4. spring
5. Groups of 4 drinks will be shown.
   One share = 4 (drinks)
6. 6, 2 7. 31, 31 8. 50 cents
9.

NOVEMBER						
Sunday	Monday	Tuesday	Wednesday	Thursday	Friday	Saturday
1	2	3	4	5	6	7
8	9	10	11	12	13	14

30.2

1. a 14 b 28
2. 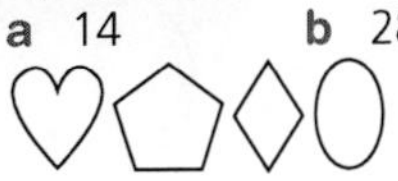
3. a 53, 

   b 93, 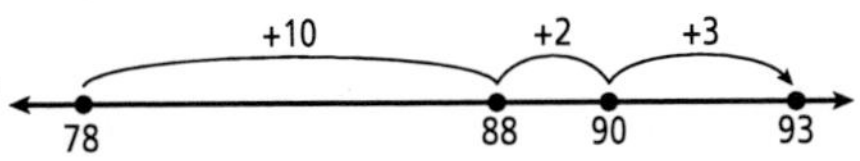

   c 48, 

   d 64, 

30.3

30c, 25c, 30c

1. a 10 cents b 70 cents c 60 cents

45 tortoises

31.1

8 + 6 = 14

1. 92 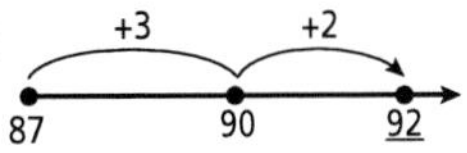

2. 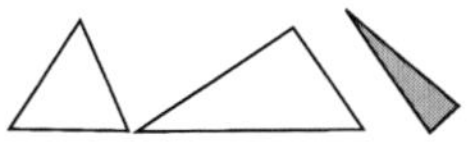
3. 2, 2 4. 4 groups of 6 = 24
5. a 15 b 5, 5 c 3, 3
6. 68 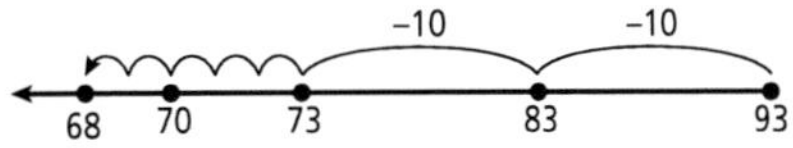

7. The triangle and square will be coloured.
8. 2, 14, 8, 16, 10, 18, 12, 6
   0, 12, 18, 20, 14, 10, 16, 4

31.2

1. Sunday, Saturday 2. a E b D c F
3. a 53 b 95 c 57

31.3

1. a $30 b $50 c $40
   d $45 e $60 f $55

55 bears

32.1

12 ÷ 2 = 6

1. 3, 3 (cans) 2. 6 (rhombuses)
3. 3 rows of 5 = 15, 3 × 5 = 15
4. 8, 8, 7, 9 5. true 6. turn
7. 6 + 6 = 12, 12
8. a 12 b 3 c 4
9. 4, 6, 8 ☒ 5

32.2

1. a 2, 2 b 6, 6 c 3, 3
   d 4, 4 e 1, 1
2. a 18 b Green c Orange

32.3

1. 26 (circles)

❷ a $\underline{26} - \underline{18} = \underline{8}$
$\underline{26} - \underline{8} = \underline{18}$

b $12 + 14 = \underline{26}$
$\underline{26} - 12 = \underline{14}$
$\underline{26} - 14 = \underline{12}$

c $15 + 11 = \underline{26}$
$\underline{26} - 15 = \underline{11}$
$\underline{26} - 11 = \underline{15}$

58 lizards

33.1

3 × 4 = 12

❶ a 23 b 29

❷ a 10, 10 b 5, 5 c 4, 4

❸ 34, 11

❹ 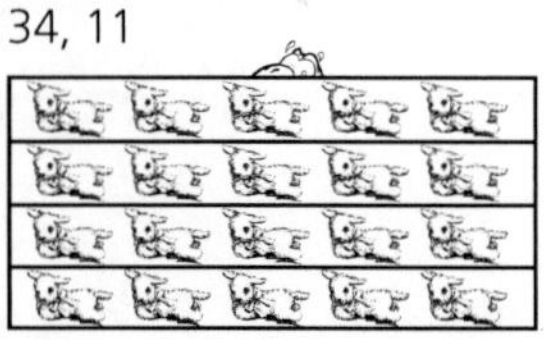
Pictures will vary.
yes

❺ flip, turn ❻ 3 out of 7 ❼ 163

❽ 10, 20, $\underline{30}$, 40, $\underline{50}$, 60, $\underline{70}$, 80, $\underline{90}$
10, 20, 30, 40, 50, 60, 70, 80
40, 60, 90, 30, 70, 50, 80, 20

33.2

1, 2, 3

❶ 

❷ a 9 b 8

33.3

❶ a 10 b 5 c 4 d 2

❷ Answers will vary.
40 on 1 floor, 20 on 2 floors, or 10 on 4 floors, 8 on 5 floors, 5 on 8 floors, 4 on 10 floors, 2 on 20 floors or 1 on 40 floors.

8 groups of seven birds = 56

34.1

9 + 4 = 13

❶ a 23 b 24 ❷ 98, 40, 15, 92

❸ 5, 10 ❹ 13, 13 ❺ 28, 9

❻ 3 out of 8, 5 out of 8

❼ edges = 12, corners = 8

❽ 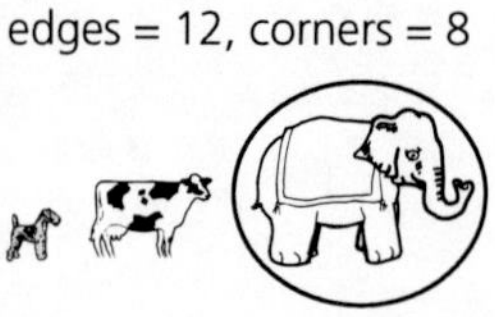

❾ a 10 b 8 c 20
d 15 e 10 f 13

34.2

4 × 2 = 8

❶ 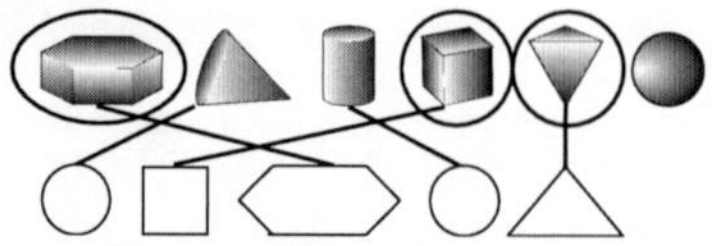

The sphere has no base.

❷ 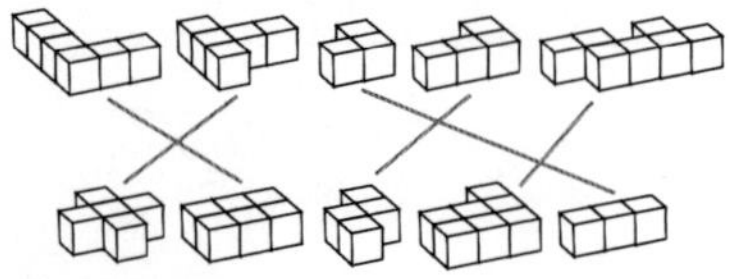

34.3

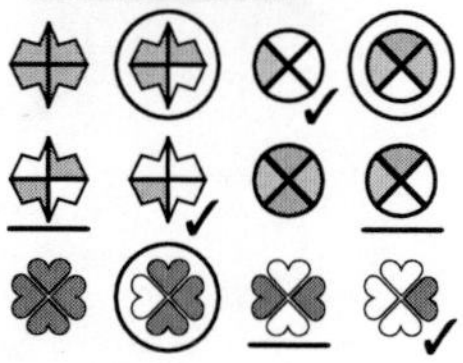

8 groups of ten caps = 80

35.1

5 × 2 = 10

❶ a 33 b 36 ❷ 15, 69, 48

❸ 6, 2, 4, 8 ❹ $1, 85c ❺ $\frac{3}{7}$

❻ 

❼ edges = 9, corners = 6 ❽ 4, 2

❾ the, cat, ate, three, mice

35.2

❶ 5, 7, 12, 16

❷ a 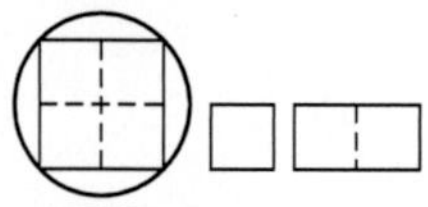

b 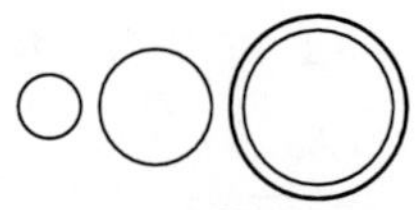

c 

d 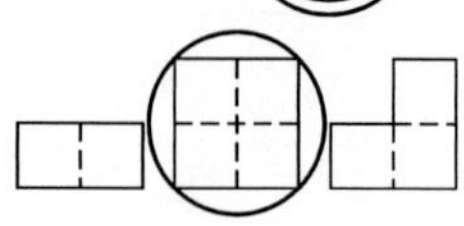

35.3

❶ 8 paperclips
❷ 3 paperclips
Answers will vary.

14 groups of four ducks = 56

Multiple-choice questions

A 41 **B** □ **C** 2 **D** 3 groups of 4
E 15 **F** 6 **G** above the bird
H 29 **I** D **J** 11

17:2

❶ Look at the pictures on the right.

a How many ducks? ____

b How many groups? ____

c How many ducks in each group? ____

d 4 × 5 = ____

❷ Look at the pictures in the heading.

a How many faces? ____

b How many faces in each group? ____

c How many groups? ____

d 3 × 4 = ____

❸

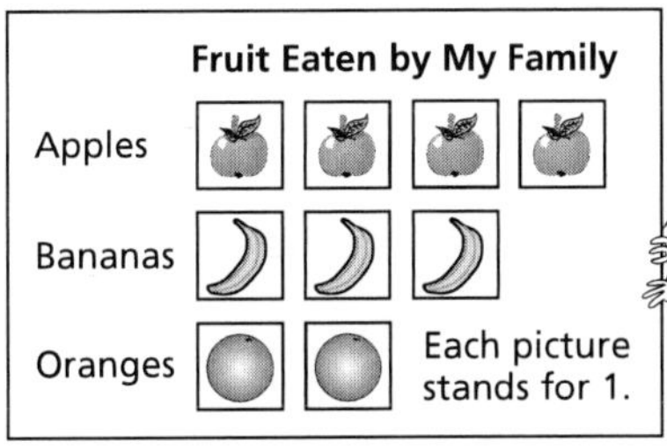

a How many bananas were eaten? ________

b How many more apples were eaten than oranges? ________

c How much fruit was eaten altogether? ________

17:3

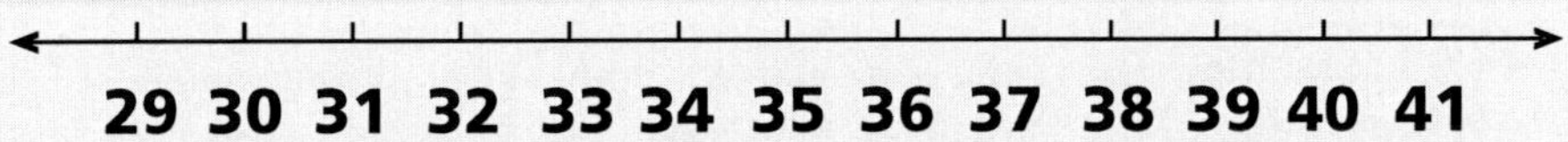

❶ Finish this pattern.

30 + 1 = 31	30 + 4 = ____	30 + 7 = ____
30 + 2 = 32	30 + 5 = ____	30 + 8 = ____
30 + 3 = ____	30 + 6 = ____	30 + 9 = ____

How many? ☐

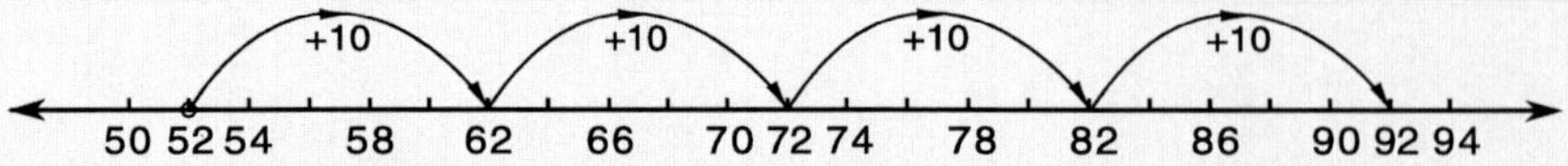

❶

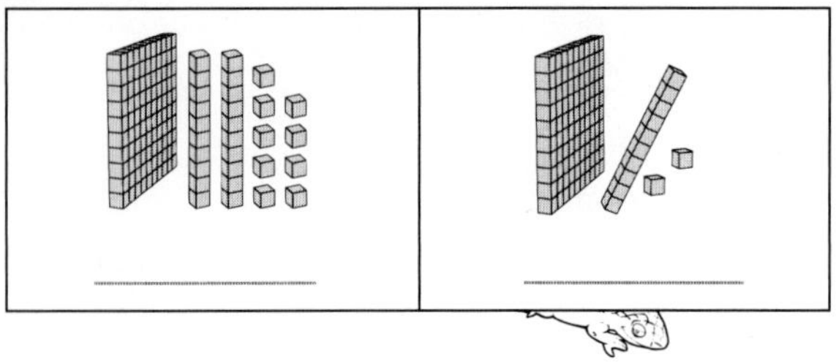

❷

3	2	9	$2
7	4	5	$1
2	6	1	$7
8	3	2	$9
+ 1	+ 8	+ 5	+ $8

❸ Colour one quarter of each.

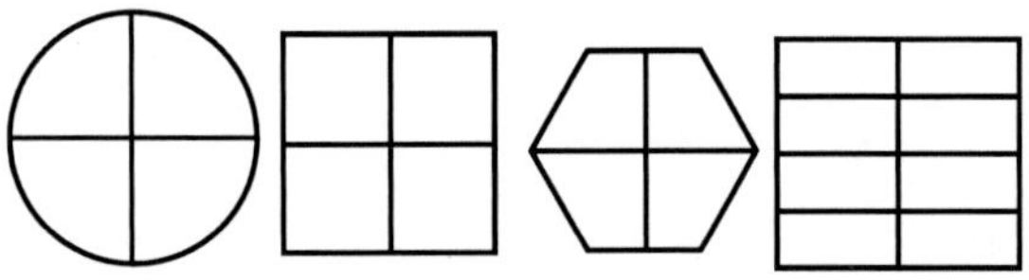

❹ 26, 36, 46, ____, ____, ____
83, 73, 63, ____, ____, ____

❺ Write the name for:

35 ______________________

❻ What fraction is coloured?

______

❼ Circle the larger number.
152 or **121**

❽ 56 + 10 = _____ 72 − 10 = _____

❾ This month is

____

❿ Colour a quarter of each group.

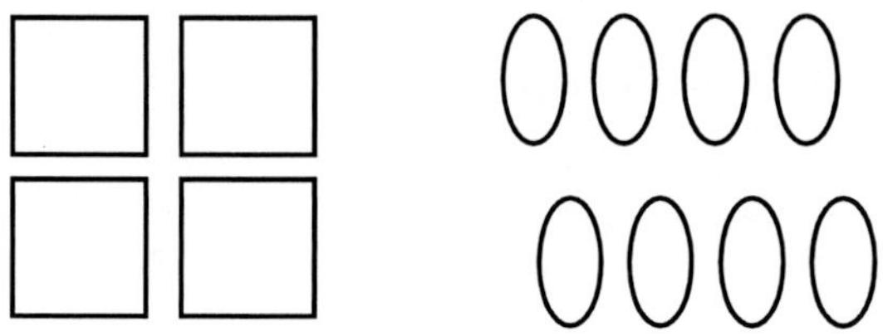

⓫ Colour $\frac{1}{2}$ of the hearts.

⓬ Complete each number web.

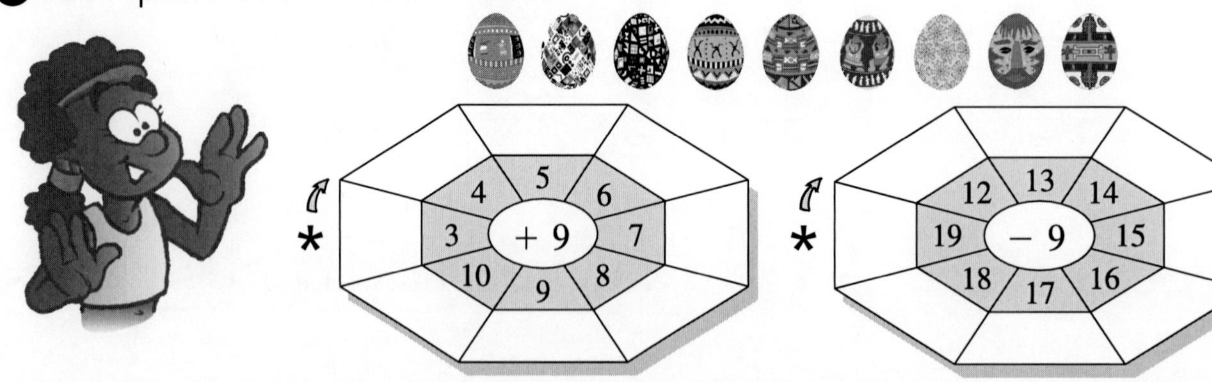

18:2 January, February, March, April, May, June, July, August, September, October, November, December

❶ We graphed the weather for one month.

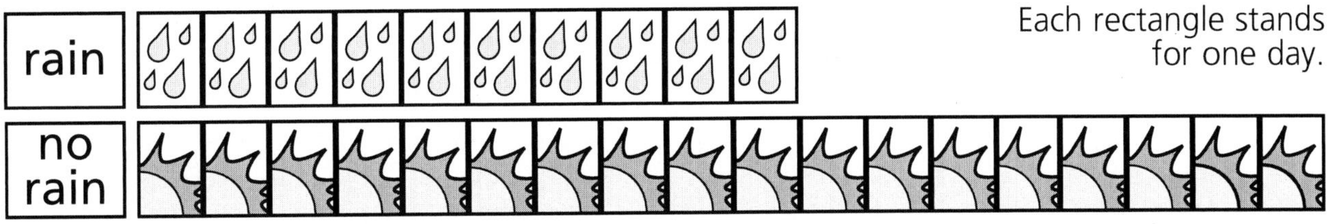

Each rectangle stands for one day.

How many days had:

a rain? ______ b no rain? ______

c How many more days had no rain than had rain? ______

d Which month did we graph? ______

❷ Show:

half past 5

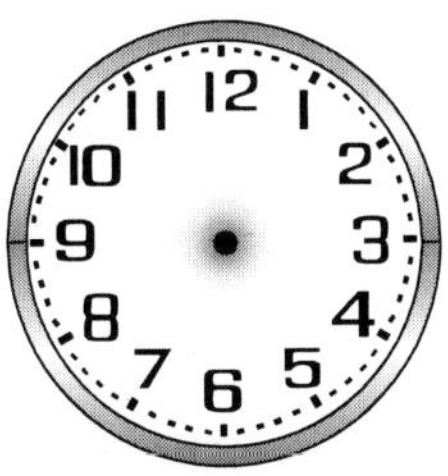

a quarter past 1

a quarter to 12

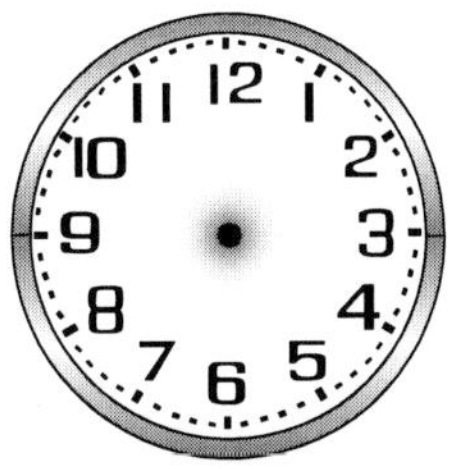

a quarter to 8

18:3

❶

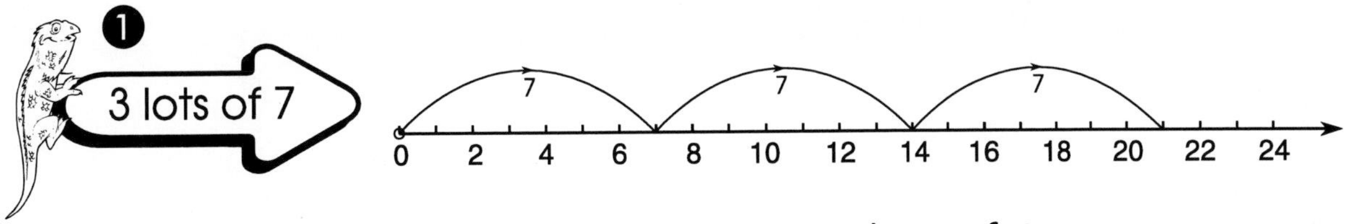

a 8 + 4 + 5 ______

b 3 lots of 8 ______

c 24 – 5 – 7 ______

d 10 + 3 + 8 ______

e 4 lots of 5 ______

f 21 – 3 – 8 ______

g 3 + 8 + 5 + 7 ______

h 4 groups of 6 ______

, ☐ - ☐ = ☐

❶ 18, 28, 38, ____, ____, ____

75, 65, 55, ____, ____, ____

❷

4 + ____ = 9   9 – 4 = ____

❸ Is it likely that you will have dinner tomorrow? ________

❹ Write 3 different number sentences.

____ + ____ =
____ + ____ =
____ + ____ =

13

❺ Name the season for March, April and May. ____________

❻ 49 + 10 = ____   81 – 10 = ____

23 + 20 = ____   67 – 30 = ____

❼ Colour the larger number in each pair.

127	179	100	172
170	180	189	170

❽ Draw lines to cut these into quarters.

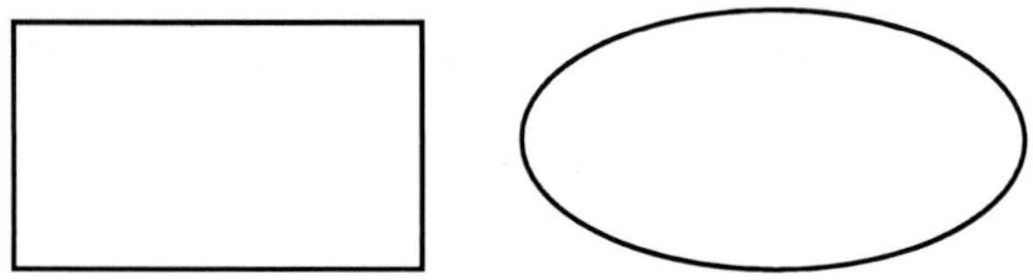

❾ Show:

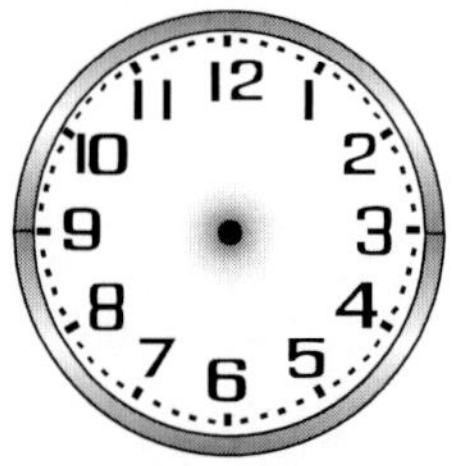

half past 3

a quarter past 11

❿ 3 → 3

Is this a flip or a slide?

____

⓫

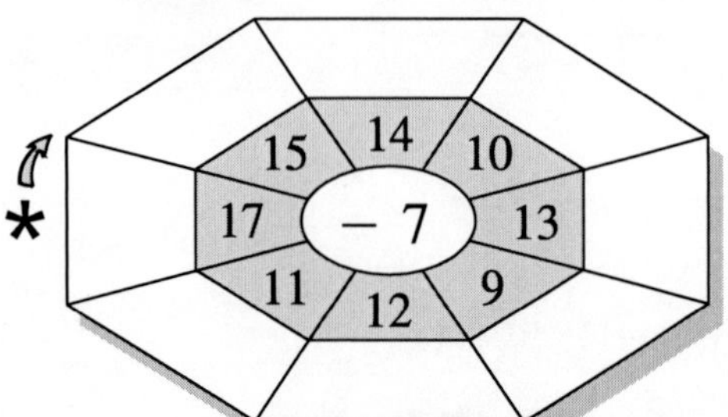

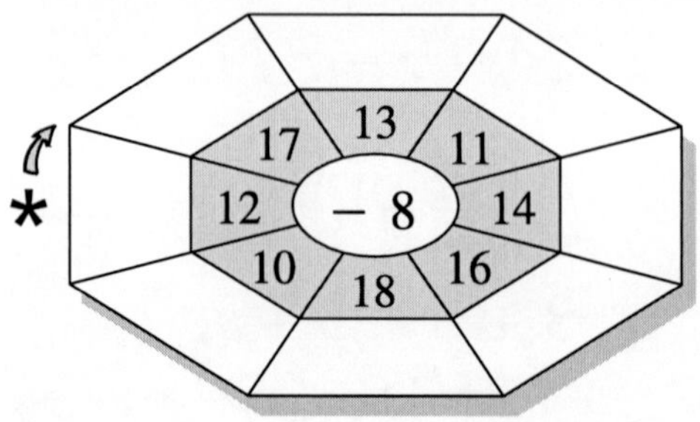

19:2

❶ Which two months come after April? ______, ______

❷ Circle the one with the smaller mass.

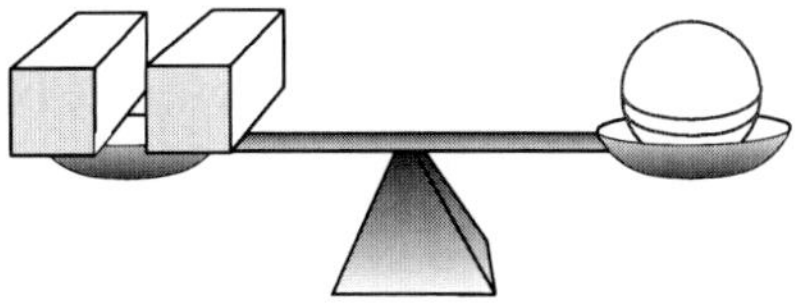

 or 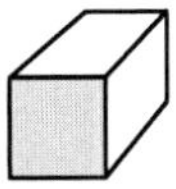

❸ The month after:

January ______ September ______

❹

+	7	5	8	6	9	4
3						
5						

	10	7	9	5	8	6
− 5						
− 3						

19:3

❶ Use the cards to answer these.

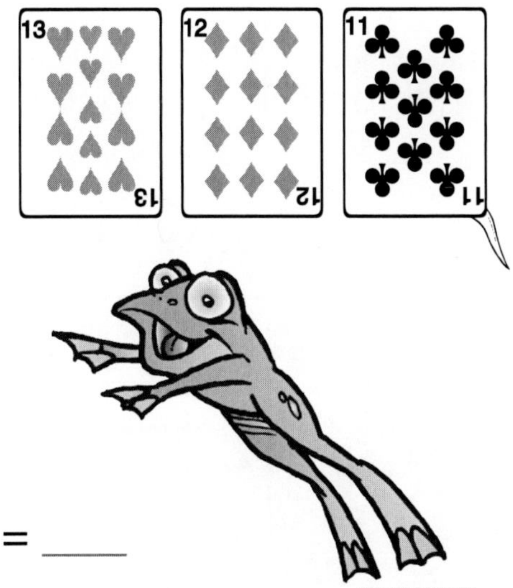

a 11 + 12 = ____ b 12 + 13 = ____

c 11 + 13 = ____ d 12 + 11 = ____

e 13 + 12 = ____ f 13 + 11 = ____

g 11 + 12 + 13 = ____ h 11 + 13 + 12 = ____

How many sheep? ☐

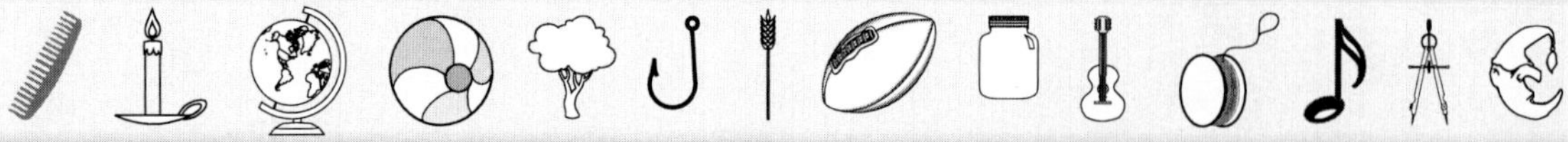

❶ 

6 + ____ = 10 10 – 4 = ____

❷ Write the number modelled.

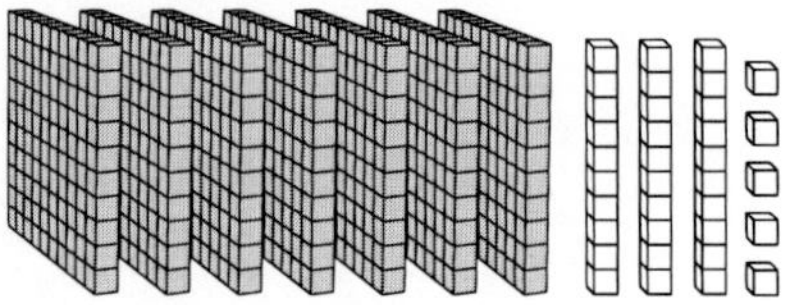

____

❸ Has the fish a greater or smaller mass than the pencil? ____________

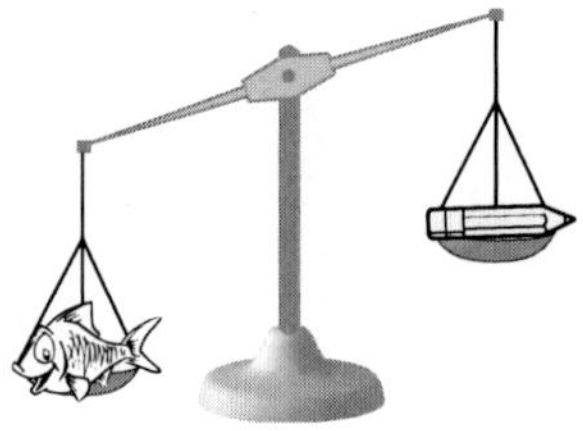

❹ Show the time.

half past 3

half past 11

❺ Circle the smallest number.

134 143 121

❻ Show:

a quarter past 9

a quarter to 7

❼ 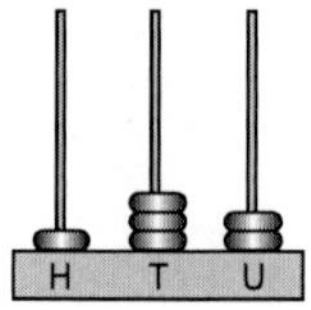

______ ______

❽ 5, 10, 15, ____, ____, ____

18, 16, 14, ____, ____, ____

4, 9, 14, ____, ____, ____

❾ The last month of the year is

____

❿ Continue these patterns by flipping or sliding across each grid.

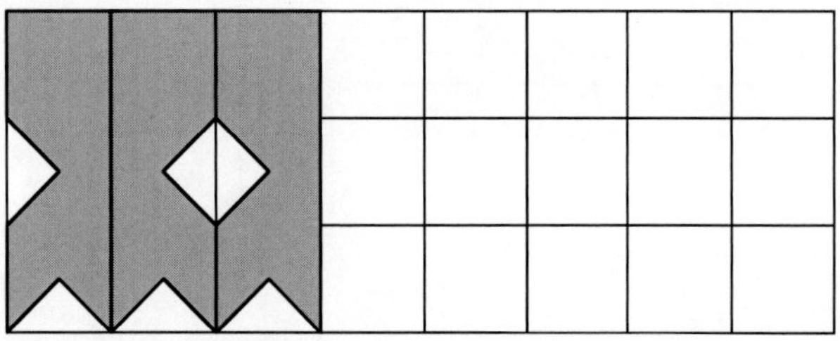

This is a **flip / slide**.

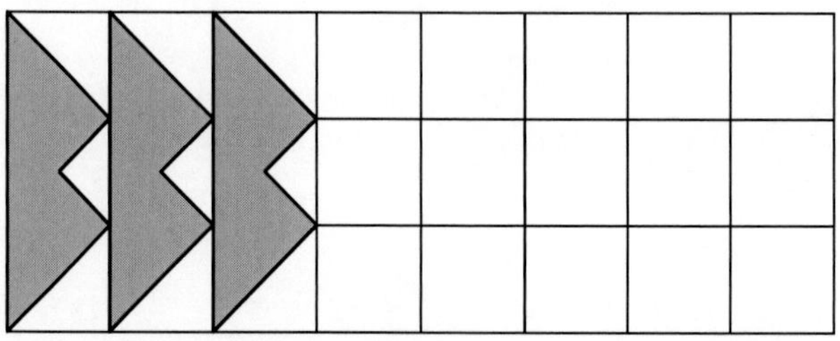

This is a **flip / slide**.

20:2

❶ What day comes after Sunday? ______________

What month is it now? ______________

❷ The ruler weighs the same as 2 pegs.
The pencil weighs the same as 3 pegs.
The plum weighs the same as 12 pegs.

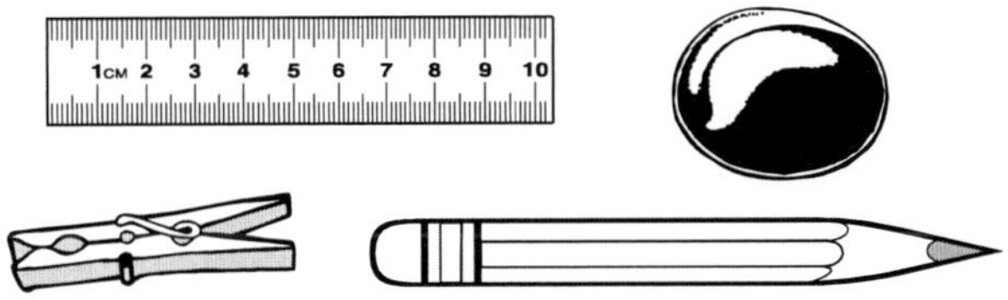

- **a** Which is the heaviest? ______________
- **b** Which is the lightest? ______________
- **c** Two pencils weigh ______ pegs.
- **d** Three pencils weigh ______ pegs.

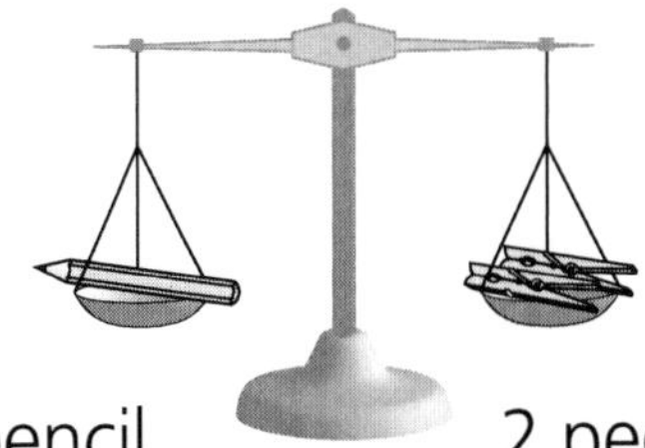

❸ **a** 5, 10, 15, ____, ____, ____, 35, ____, ____, 50, ____

b 0, 10, 20, ____, ____, ____, 60, ____, ____, 90, ____

20:3

Shade all parts that show a slide. Leave the flips and turns as they are.

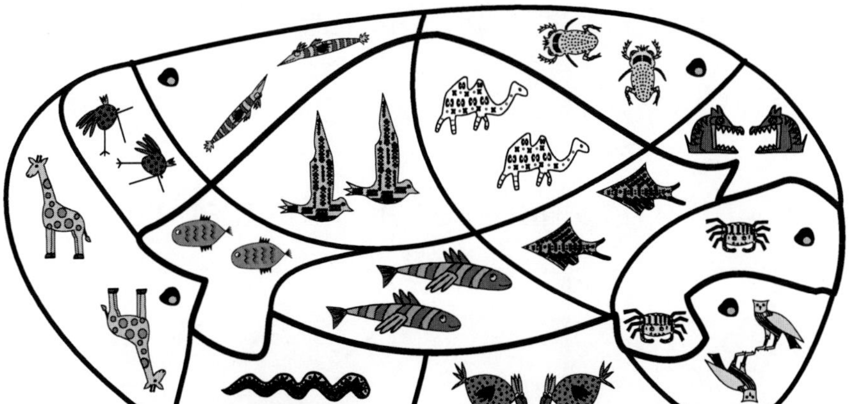

☐ groups of five rabbits = ☐

❶

2 + ______ = 10

______ + 8 = 10

10 − ______ = 2

10 − ______ = 8

❷ Write the number modelled.

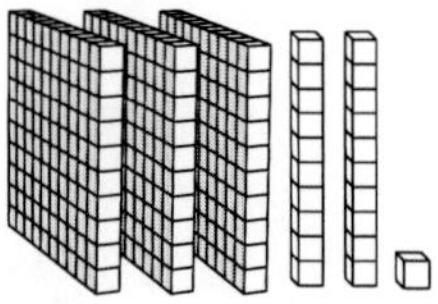

 ______

❸ How much altogether?

______ c

❹ Colour the shape with the greatest area.

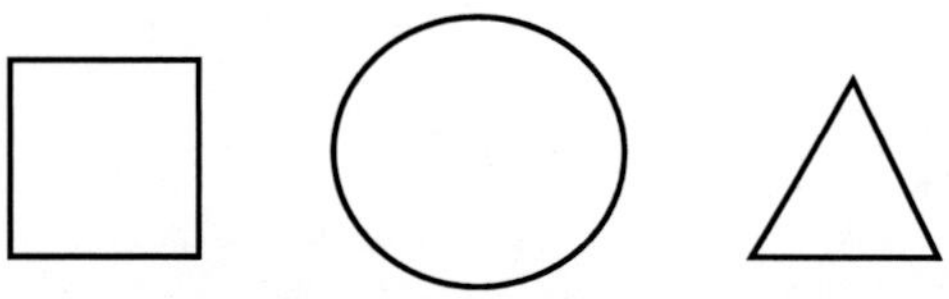

❺ 40, 45, 50, ______, ______

33, 43, 53, ______, ______

❻ What is the name of the month at the beginning of the year?

____

❼ **a** What is the area of this shape?

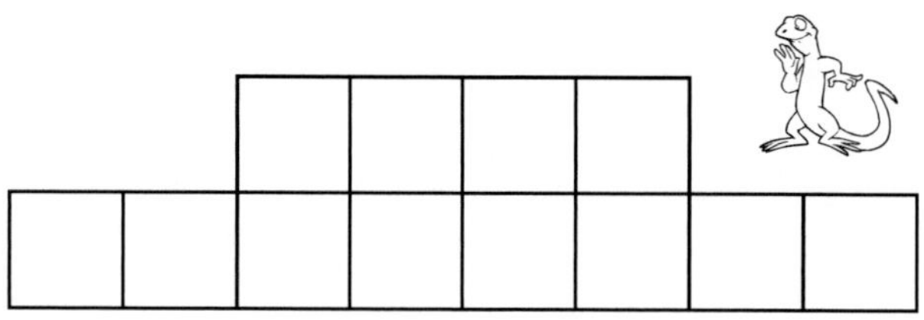

Area = ______ squares

b Colour half of the squares red.

❽ How many days in 1 week? ______

❾ Write the numerals for:

seventeen ______

twenty-nine ______

❿ Colour the hexagons red and the triangles blue.

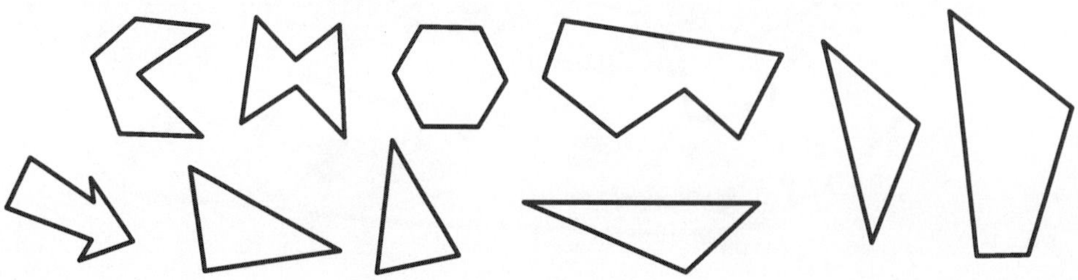

21:2

 , ☐ **groups of** ☐ **=** ☐

1. Circle the coins with a value of less than 20 cents.
Colour the silver coins grey and the gold coin yellow.

2. Draw a shape with a:

smaller area than 

larger area than 

3. Put a cross **under** the table.
Draw a star **above** the table.
Draw a chair to the **right** of the table.
Put a ball in the **middle** of the table.

21:3

 = ☐

1. Write four number sentences for each total.

___ + ___ + ___ + ___ =
___ + ___ + ___ + ___ =
___ + ___ + ___ + ___ =
___ + ___ + ___ + ___ =

16

___ + ___ + ___ + ___ =
___ + ___ + ___ + ___ =
___ + ___ + ___ + ___ =
___ + ___ + ___ + ___ =

20

☐ groups of four ants = ☐

 • *AUSTRALIAN SIGNPOST MATHS 2 MENTALS* • ISBN 978 1 4886 2180 2

☐ cones

❶ 9 + 7 = ____ 16 – 7 = ____

7 + ____ = 16 16 – ____ = 7

❷

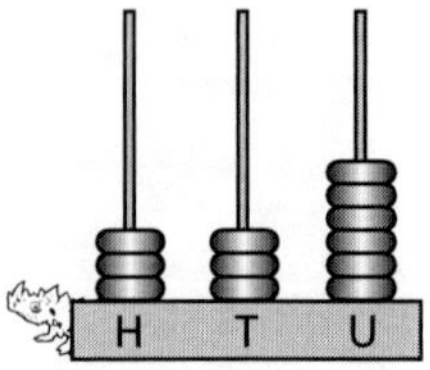

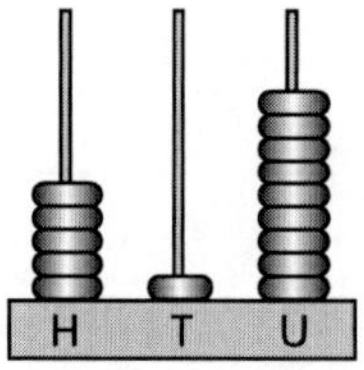

________ ________

❸ How much money is shown here?

______

❹ Write the area of each shape.

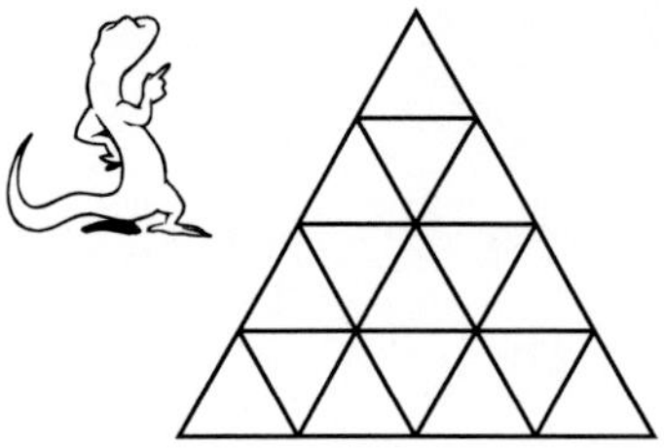

____ triangles ____ diamonds

❺ Circle 3 groups of 8 cones above.

How many groups of 4 cones would there be? ______

❻ Draw a parallelogram on the right side of this trapezium.

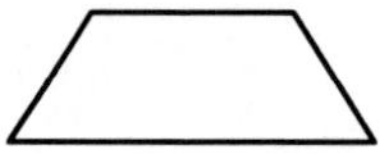

❼

____ groups of ____ = ____

____ × ____ = ____

❽ Show how you could make 20 cents using 4 coins.

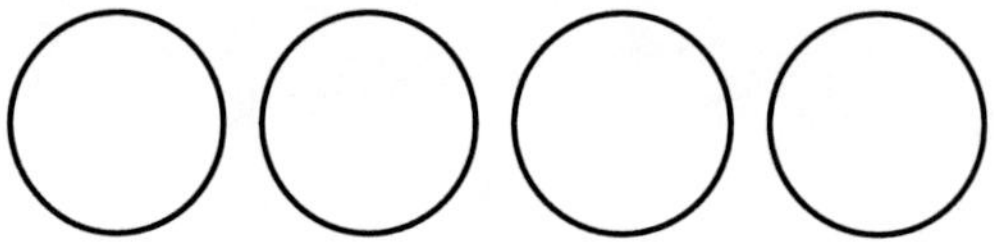

❾ Complete each number web.

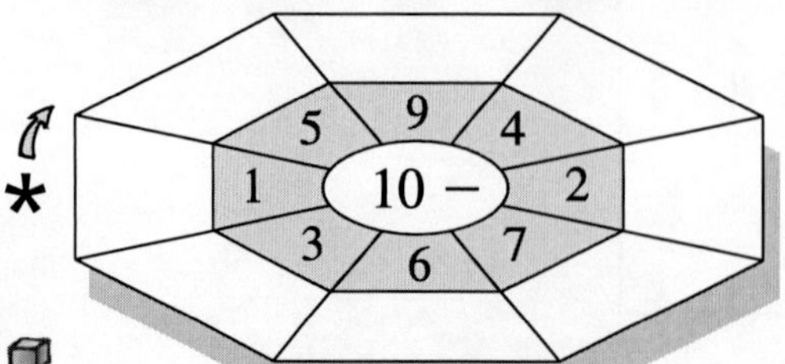

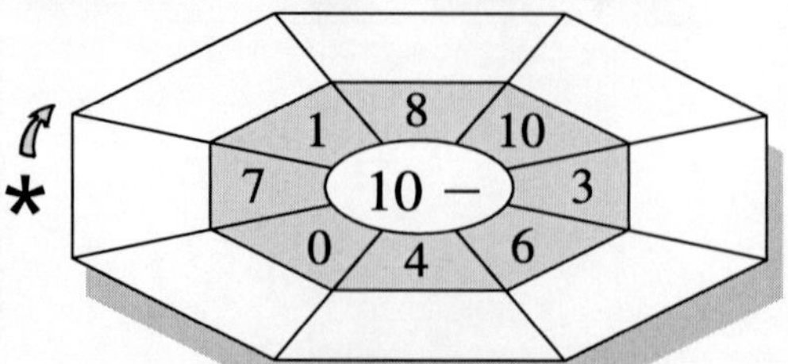

 ISBN 978 1 4886 2180 2

22:2

 , ☐ × 3 = ☐ **blocks**

❶ Colour the coins that make 60c.

❷ Colour 2 shapes that fit together to make the rectangle.

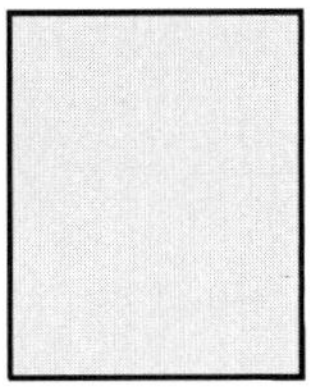

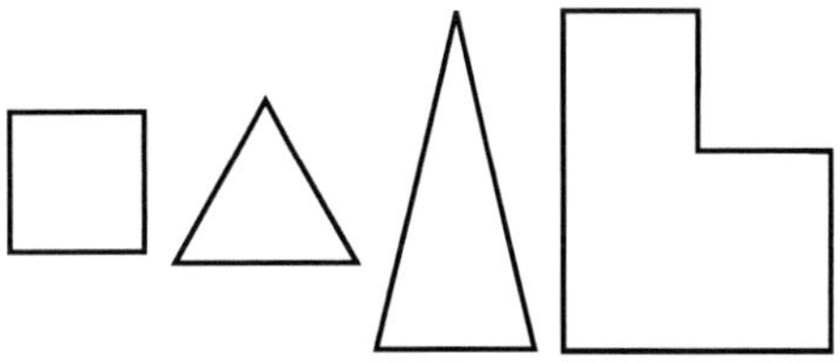

❸ Draw a ball **between** the girl and boy and a cloud **behind** the girl.

22:3

 , ☐ × ☐ = ☐

❶ How many bolts will balance:

- **a** a globe and a lock? ______
- **b** a torch and a candle? ______
- **c** two candles? ______
- **d** six torches? ______

How many globes will balance:

- **e** a candle? ______
- **f** a torch? ______

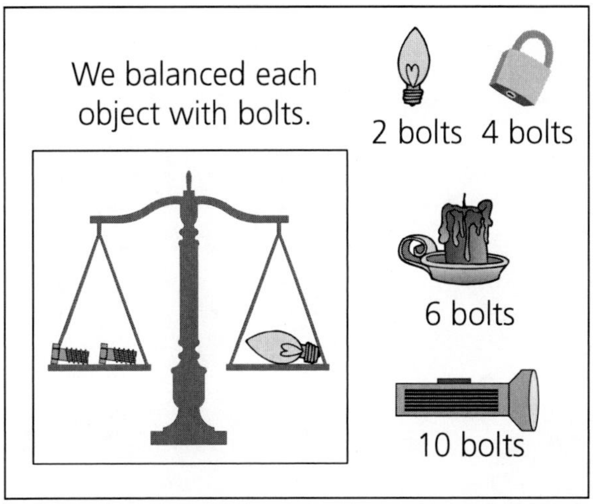

How many camels? ☐

 • *AUSTRALIAN SIGNPOST MATHS 2 MENTALS* • ISBN 978 1 4886 2180 2

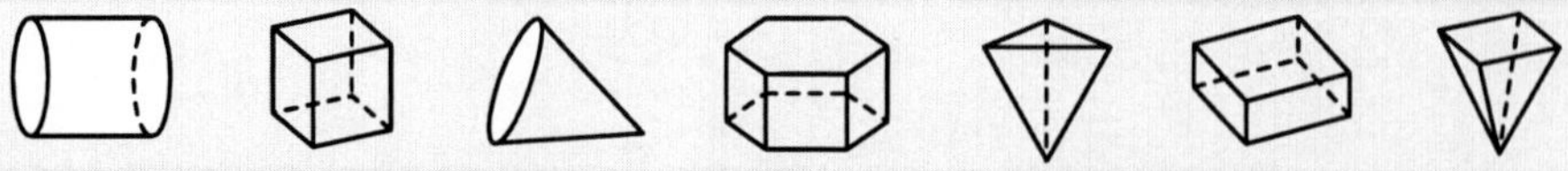

❶ What number is shown here?

______

❷ Draw a parallelogram.
How many:
sides? ______
corners? ______

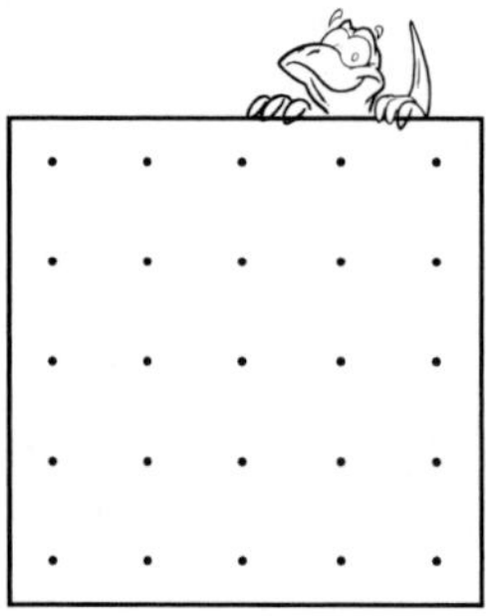

❸

4×2 horns = ______ horns

____ + ____ + ____ + ____ = ____

❹ Which shape has the greatest area? ______

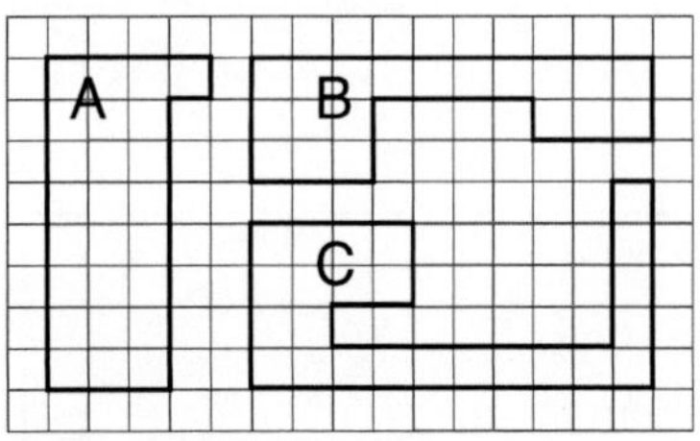

❺ **a** Is this a hexagon?

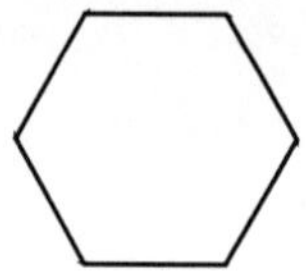

______

b How many sides does it have? ______

❻ Answer these sums (by bridging to tens).

18 + 6 = ____ 29 + 4 = ____

❼ Double 3

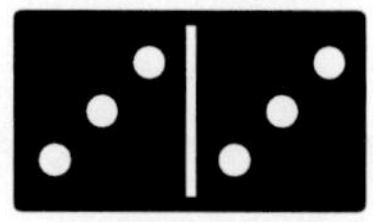

______ + ______ = ______

2 × ______ = ______

❽ Show how you could make 60 cents using 4 coins.

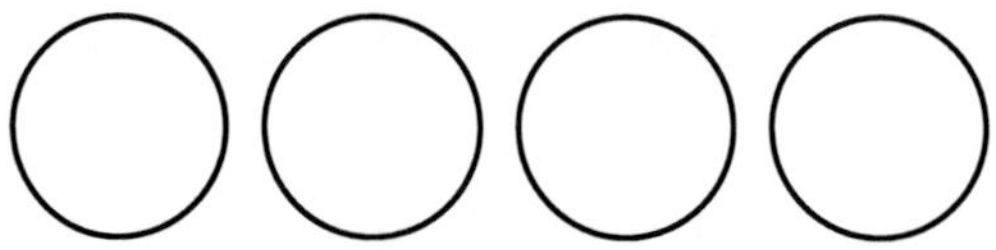

❾

a	b	c	d
\$ 7 + \$ 3 = ______	\$ 10 + \$ 5 = ______	\$ 4 + \$ 8 = ______	\$ 6 + \$ 5 = ______

e	f	g	h
\$ 11 − \$ 4 = ______	\$ 12 − \$ 8 = ______	\$ 13 − \$ 5 = ______	\$ 16 − \$ 7 = ______

23:2

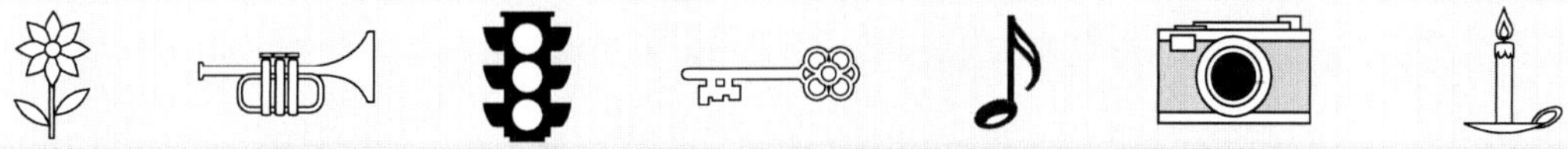

❶ Copy each object and draw a line to match it with its name.

cone   cylinder   cube   prism

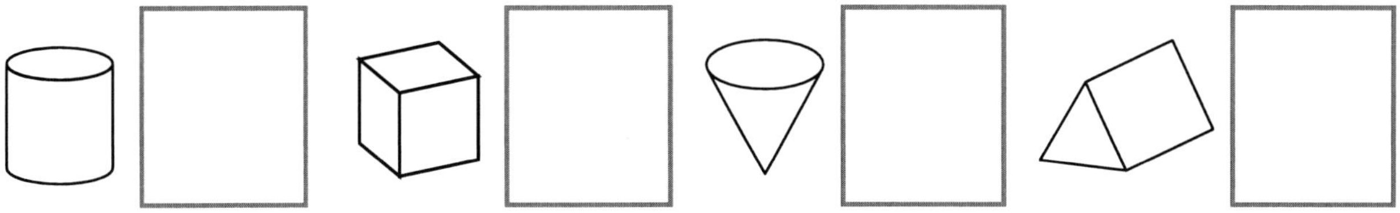

❷

14	19	11	15	18
− 8	− 5	− 6	− 0	− 9
____	____	____	____	____

❸

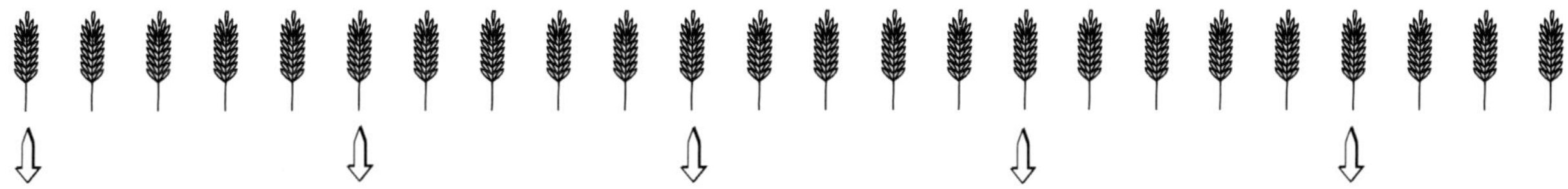

1st   ______   ______   ______   ______

23:3

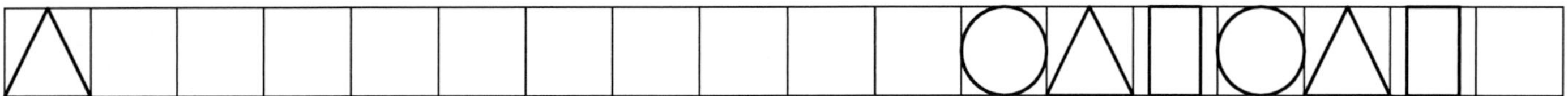

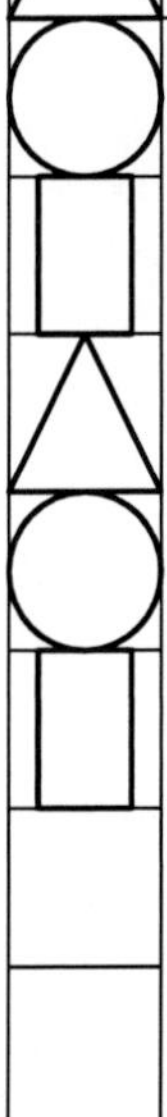

❶ Use the number line to complete these.

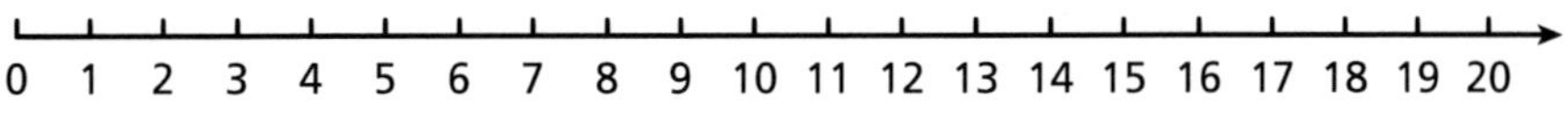

a 19 − ____ = 7   **b** 17 − ____ = 8   **c** 15 − 8 = ____

d 16 − ____ = 8   **e** 14 − ____ = 5   **f** 19 − ____ = 11

g 18 − ____ = 5   **h** 19 − 5 = ____   **i** 18 − ____ = 14

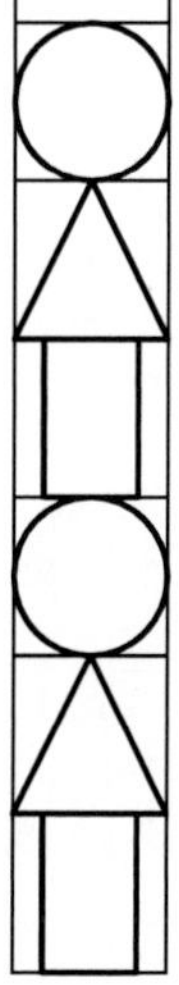

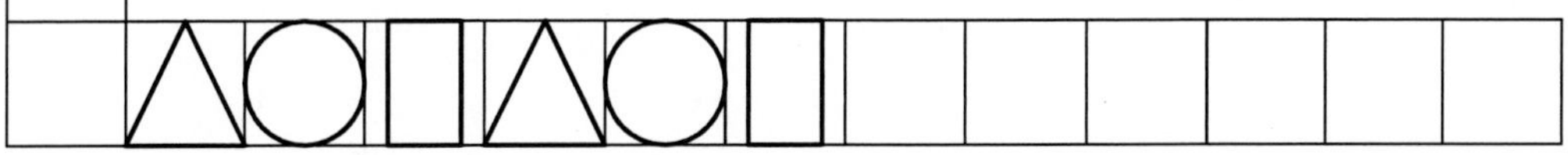

Complete this pattern.

24:1

, ☐ × ☐ = ☐

1

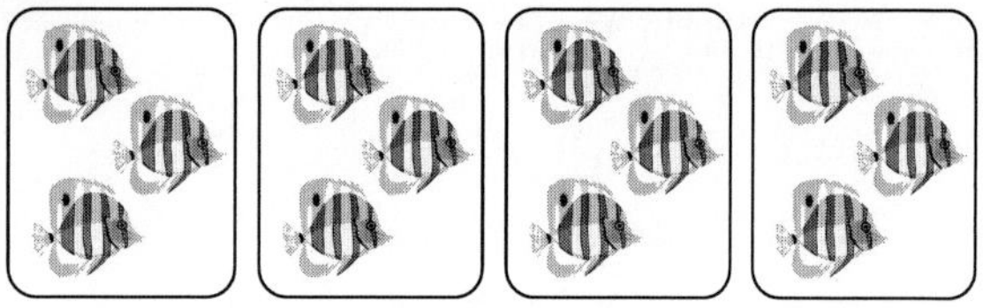

____ groups of ____ = ____

____ + ____ + ____ + ____ = ____

____ × ____ = ____

2 What number does this tally show?  ______

3 Answer these sums (by bridging to tens).

79 + 4 = _____   18 + 5 = _____

4

_____ groups of _____ = _____

_____ × _____ = _____

5

What is the total value? _____

6

______   ______

7

10 cents + 10 cents = ________

Half of 20 cents = ________

A quarter of 20 cents = ________

8 Write the words for:

40 ______________________

70 ______________________

30 ______________________

51	52	53	54	55	56	57	58	59	60
61	62	63	64	65	66	67	68	69	70
71	72	73	74	75	76	77	78	79	80
81	82	83	84	85	86	87	88	89	90
91	92	93	94	95	96	97	98	99	100

9

a 57 + 10 = ____

b 72 + 10 = ____

c 89 + 10 = ____

d 10 + 81 = ____

e 10 + 58 = ____

f 10 + 90 = ____

 ISBN 978 1 4886 2180 2

24:2

❶ Draw these objects.

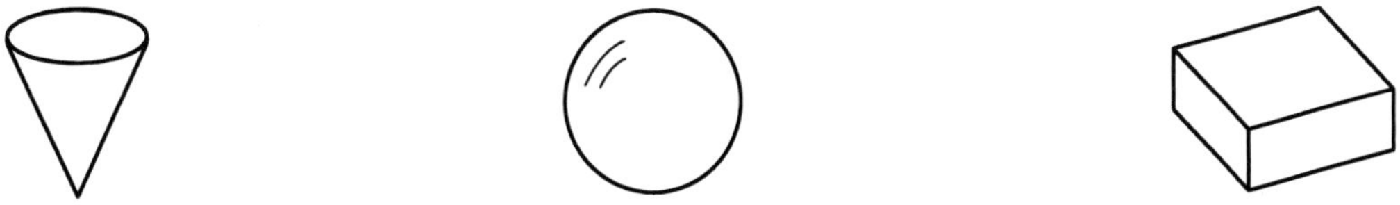

❷ Use the pictures to finish the graph.

Lives in Trees							
Lives on Land							
Lives in Water							

24:3

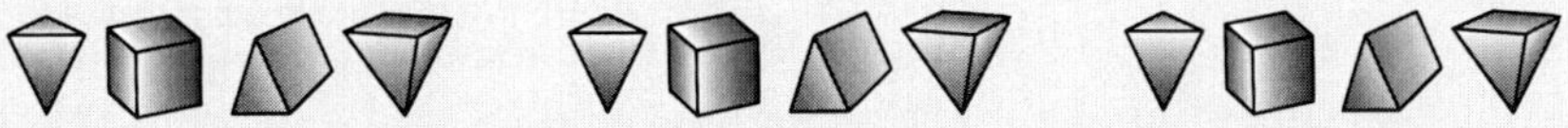

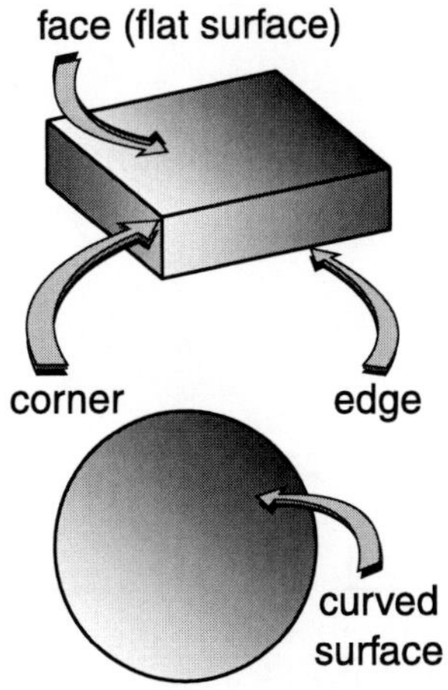

❶ Use words to describe each object.

a 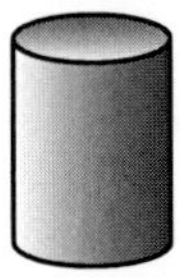

____ faces

____ edges

____ curved surface

b 

____ faces

____ edges

____ corners

c 

____ face

____ edge

____ curved surface

☐ groups of five paw prints = ☐

, ☐ - ☐ = ☐

1. Double 8 = ____ + ____ = ____

   2 × 8 = ____

2. 13 subtract 8. ______

3. Draw a picture that you have cut into halves. Cut it in half.

4. Colour $\frac{1}{4}$ of these insects.

5. This is a tally. What number does it represent? 卌 ____

6. Answer these sums (by bridging to tens).

   77 + 5 = ____   39 + 3 = ____

7. 15, 25, 35, ____ , ____

   6, 8, 10, ____ , ____

   65, 60, 55, ____ , ____

8. What is the total value? ________

9. 

   ______ groups of ______ cats

   = ______ cats altogether.

   3 × 8 = ______

10. Complete each table.

    Each stroke stands for one. A gate stands for five.

a

Object	Tally	Number
pens	||||	4
pots	卌 卌 ||	
cups	卌 |||	

b

Object	Tally	Number
hats	卌 卌 ||	
dogs	卌 卌 卌	
hens	卌 卌 卌 |	

 • *AUSTRALIAN SIGNPOST MATHS 2 MENTALS* • ISBN 978 1 4886 2180 2

25:2

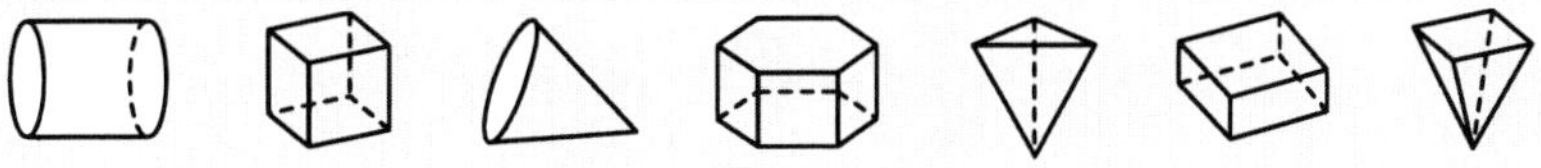

❶ Circle the coins that will add to give the value of the first coin.

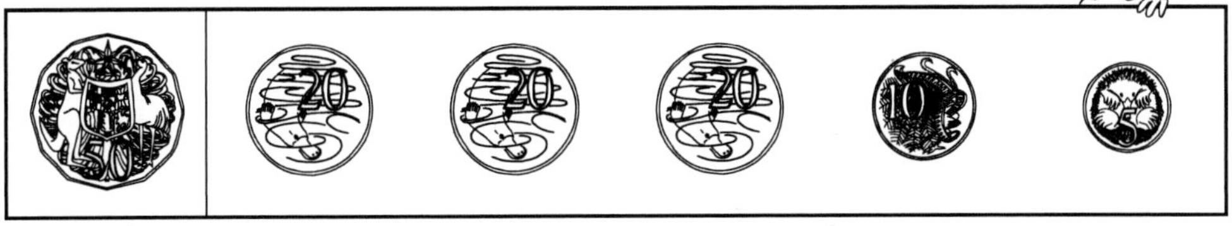

❷ **Bikes Sold**

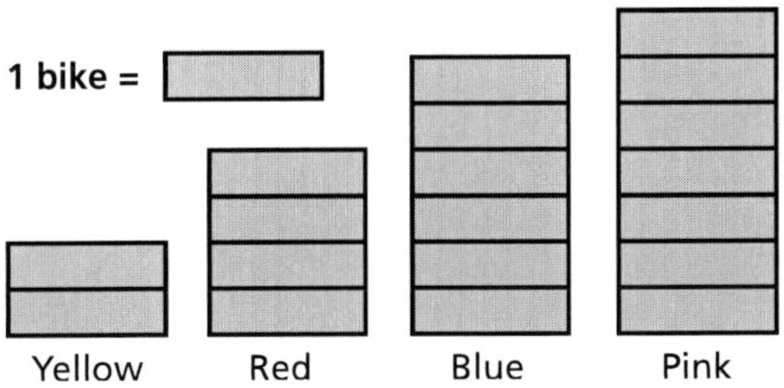

a The most popular colour. ______________

b The least popular colour. ______________

c How many red bikes were sold? ______________

d How many bikes sold altogether? ______________

25:3

Mass	 2 bolts	 4 bolts	 6 bolts	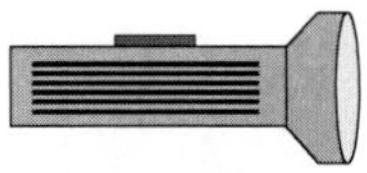 10 bolts

❶ Which is heavier:

a 3 globes or a lock? ______________

b 2 locks or a torch? ______________

c 5 globes or 2 locks? ______________

d 2 candles or 3 locks? ______________

How many worms? ☐

 , ___ - ___ = ___

1 

___ groups of ___ = ___

___ × ___ = ___

2 Round off to the nearest 10.

23 ___ 38 ___ 75 ___

3 Use this list to complete the graph and table.

List:

1, 4, 2, 3, 4, 1, 4, 3, 4, 1

Graph:

1	2	3	4

Table:

1	
2	
3	
4	

4 What numbers are shown here?

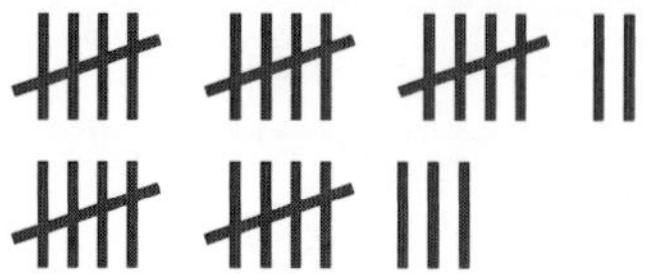

___

___

5 90, 80, 70, ___ , ___

35, 40, 45, ___ , ___

6 Colour $\frac{1}{8}$.

7 Double 10 = ___ + ___ = ___

2 × 10 = ___

8 77 = ___ tens ___ ones

9 How many tens in 90? ___

10 Write the numeral and words for each number shown.

a 4 hundreds 3 tens 2 ones ☐ ___

b 2 hundreds 9 tens 4 ones ☐ ___

c 7 hundreds 0 tens 5 ones ☐ ___

 • *AUSTRALIAN SIGNPOST MATHS 2 MENTALS* • ISBN 978 1 4886 2180 2

26:2

eagles

❶ How much money?

a  ______

b  ______

c  ______

d  ______

e  ______

f  ______

❷ I am standing at X.
Where will I be if I move:

a 1 left then
4 forward? ______

b 5 forward, 2 right
then 5 down? ______

front

D		G		
	F		H	
	C			
			E	
A				
		X		B

26:3

❶ Write the time in words and numerals.

quarter past ten

10 : 15

quarter

a 

______

:

b 

______

:

c 

______

:

☐ groups of three lizards = ☐

27:1

 , ☐ × ☐ = ☐

1

How many groups? ______

How many toys? ______

6 × 3 = ______

2 Round off to the nearest 10.

97 ______ 55 ______

3 Use the split strategy to find:

21 + 17 = ______

26 + 12 = ______

4 This month is ______________.

Last month was ______________.

Next month is ______________.

5 Colour $\frac{1}{2}$ of the circles.

○ ○ ○ ○ ○ ○

6 Double 7 = ____ + ____ = ____

2 × 7 = ____

7 Use this list to complete the graph and table.

List: yes, no, no, yes, no, no

Graph:

yes	no

Table:

yes	
no	

8 Use the split strategy to find:

63 – 22 = ______

84 – 13 = ______

9

91	92		94		96		98	99	
101		103		105		107		109	110
			114		116	117			
	122		124	125		127	128		
131		133		135	136		138	139	

 ISBN 978 1 4886 2180 2

27:2

𝍸 | ☐ , 𝍸 ||| ☐ , 𝍸 || ☐

1

2 groups of 5 equals ______

______ × ______ = ______

2

3 groups of 4 equals ______

______ × ______ = ______

3 Name the months in:

spring ____________________

summer ____________________

autumn ____________________

winter ____________________

27:3

1 Draw two coins in each money box to make:

fifteen cents = 

a twenty-five cents

b forty cents

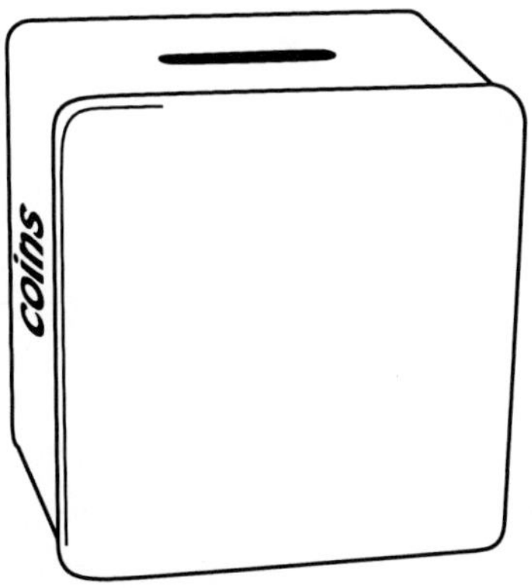

28:1

 , ☐ × ☐ = ☐

❶ 

_____ groups of _____ = _____

_____ × _____ = _____

❷ How much money altogether?

_____ cents

❸ This is a p __________.

It has ends that are the same shape and sides that are rectangles.

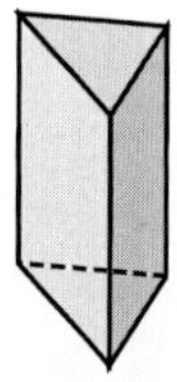

❹ Circle: December, January and February are in

summer / **spring**.

❺ Use the split strategy to find:

66 + 21 = ___   83 + 15 = ___

58 – 31 = ___   64 – 21 = ___

❻ Is it likely that you will sleep tonight? _______

❼ 50 = _____ tens _____ ones

❽ Copy this trapezium.

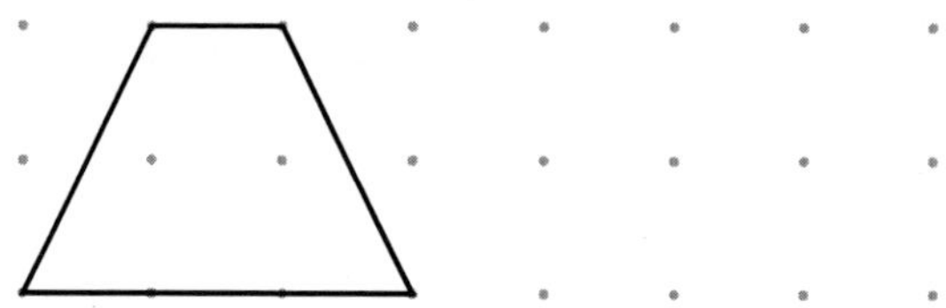

❾ What season has the months September, October and November?

____

❿ Circle: It is **likely** / **unlikely** that you will see the sun this week.

⓫ Name these shapes.

Learn ID Cards A and B on pages 4 and 5.

a  __________

b 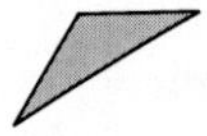 __________

c  __________

d  __________

e 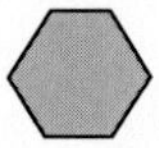 __________

f  __________

g 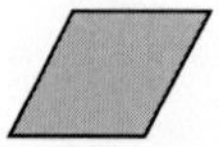 __________

h  __________

28:2

 , ☐ × ☐ = ☐

❶ Match each picture with its correct number sentence.

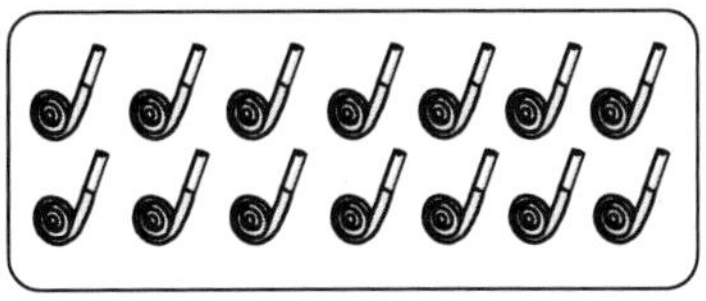 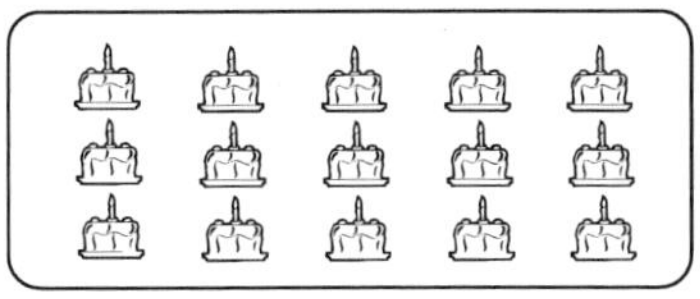 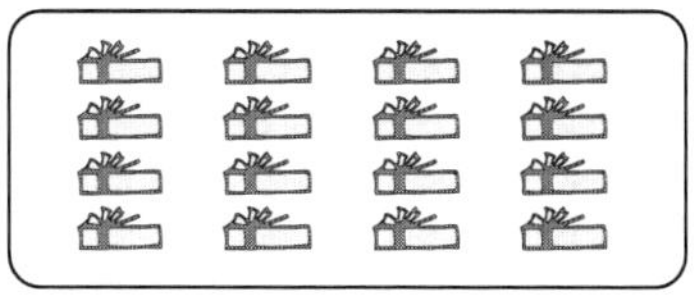

$3 \times 5 = 15$ $4 \times 4 = 16$ $2 \times 7 = 14$

❷ Use the split strategy to answer these sums.

32 + 43 = ________ 61 + 24 = ________ 72 + 25 = ________

❸ Circle the summer pictures.

28:3

 ☐ + ☐ = ☐

❶ What is the value of each group of coins?

5c 5c 5c = ______ cents 5c 5c 5c 5c = ______ cents

20c 10c 5c = ______ cents 10c 10c 10c 10c = ______ cents

20c 20c 20c = ______ cents 20c 20c 20c 20c = ______ cents

☐ 20c 5c 5c = ______ cents 20c 10c 10c 5c = ______ cents ☐

 ☐

29:1 **127, 128, ______ , ______ , 131, ______ , 133**

❶ Match each word to a picture.

prism
cylinder

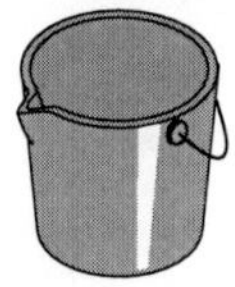

❷ Circle: It is **likely / unlikely** that you will eat tomorrow.

❸ Copy this parallelogram.

❹ Today is ______________.

Yesterday was ______________.

❺ Circle the shape with the smallest area.

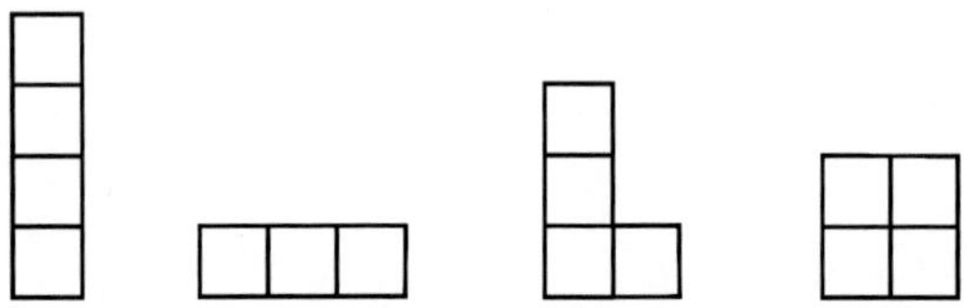

❻ Use the split strategy to find:

35 + 21 = ______

63 + 11 = ______

❼ Draw coins to make 65c.

❽ Share these among 3 boys.

One share = ______

❾ In Question 8, how many boys could be given:

3 cupcakes? ______

2 cupcakes? ______

❿ **a** *January, February, ________, ________, ________, June*
________, August, September, October, November, ________

b Months in a year? ______ **c** Months in 2 years? ______

Days in: **d** April? ______ **e** October? ______ **f** September? ______

g Circle the 8th month of the year.

h Put a cross on the 11th month of the year.

 ISBN 978 1 4886 2180 2

29:2

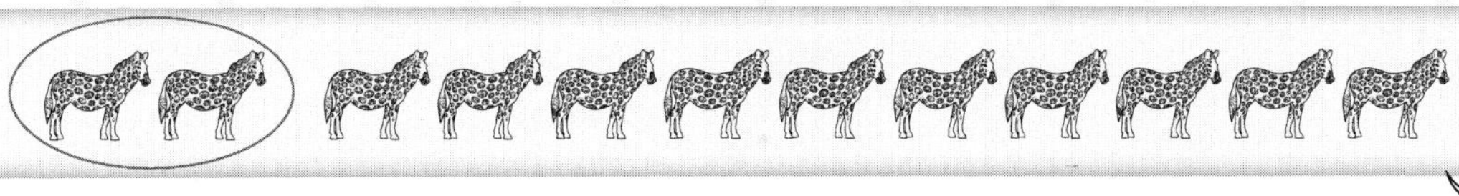

❶ Name these shapes.

h________ p________ r________ t________

❷ There are ______ days in one week.

The day after Wednesday is ________________.

❸ Write the next ordinal number after:

18th ______ 23rd ______ 21st ______ 29th ______

❹ Would it take a minute, an hour or a day to make a cake?

____

29:3

❶ Draw coins worth:

15 cents	(10c) (5c)	35 cents	◯ ◯ ◯
25 cents	◯ ◯	45 cents	◯ ◯ ◯
30 cents	◯ ◯	60 cents	◯ ◯ ◯
40 cents	◯ ◯	70 cents	◯ ◯ ◯ ◯

30:1

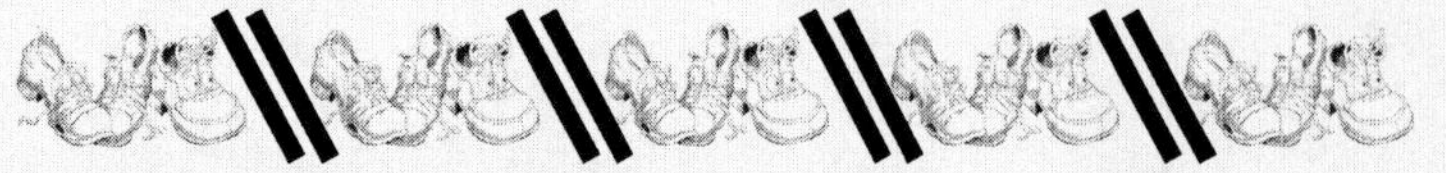 , ☐ × ☐ = ☐

1. Circle the activity that takes longer than 1 hour.

2. List all the possible outcomes if you rolled one dice.

____

3. Draw 2 groups of 3 stars.

☐ ☐

_____ groups of _____ = _____

4. Circle: September, October and November are in **autumn / spring**.

5. Show 3 equal shares.

One share = _____

6. In Question 5, how many people could be given:

2 drinks? ________

6 drinks? ________

7. How many days in:

December? ______

May? ______

8. How much money?

______ cents

9. Fill in the calendar for November for the first 2 weeks.

NOVEMBER 						
Sunday	Monday	Tuesday	Wednesday	Thursday	Friday	Saturday
1						

 • *AUSTRALIAN SIGNPOST MATHS 2 MENTALS* • ISBN 978 1 4886 2180 2

30:2

1 a How many days in 2 weeks? ______

b How many days in 4 weeks? ______

2 1st 

Draw the shape in the position:

6th ☐ 2nd ☐ 9th ☐ 8th ☐

3 Use the jump strategy to find:

a 49 + 4 = ______

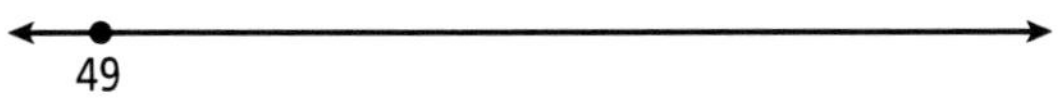

b 78 + 15 = ______

c 54 – 6 = ______

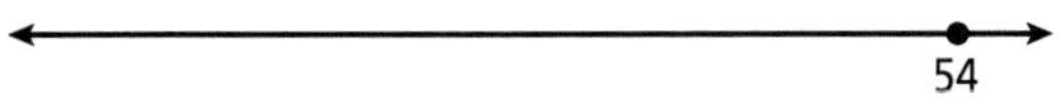

d 81 – 17 = ______

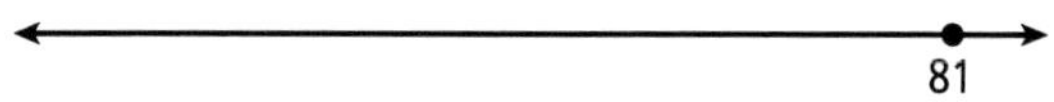

30:3

10c 20c ☐ , 5c 20c ☐ , 10c 10c 10c ☐

1 Write the total cost in each case.

a 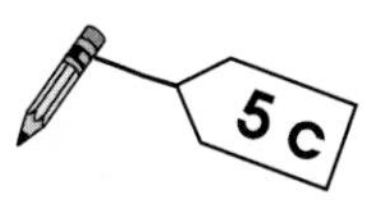

and 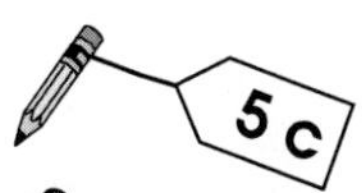

= ______ cents

b 

and 

= ______ cents

c 

and 

= ______ cents

How many? ☐

© PEARSON AUSTRALIA 2018 • *AUSTRALIAN SIGNPOST MATHS 2 MENTALS* • ISBN 978 1 4886 2180 2

31:1

$\square + \square = \square$

❶ Use the jump strategy to find

87 + 5 = ______

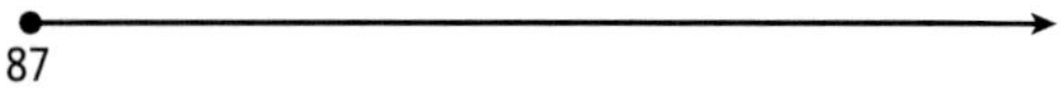

❷ Colour the triangle with the smallest area.

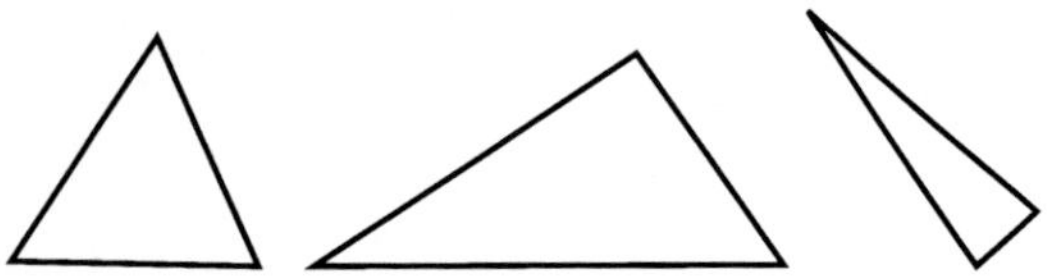

❸ Share 10 stars among 5.

10 ÷ 5 = ______

Each has ______ .

❹ 4 groups of _____ = _____

❺ 

a How many fish? ______

How many:

b groups of 3? ______

15 ÷ 3 = ______

c groups of 5? ______

15 ÷ 5 = ______

❻ Use the jump strategy to find

93 – 25 = ______

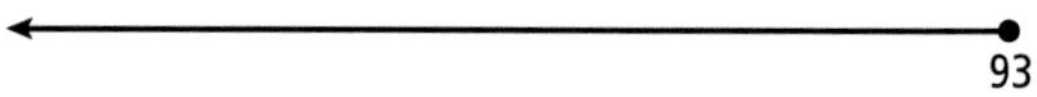

❼ Colour the two shapes that could fill the shaded area.

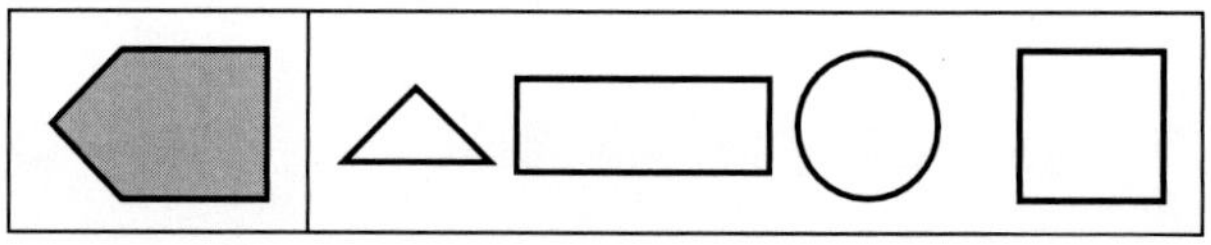

❽ Complete each number web.

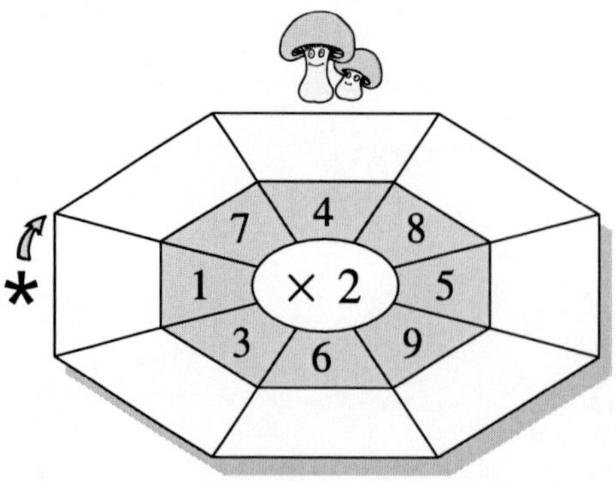

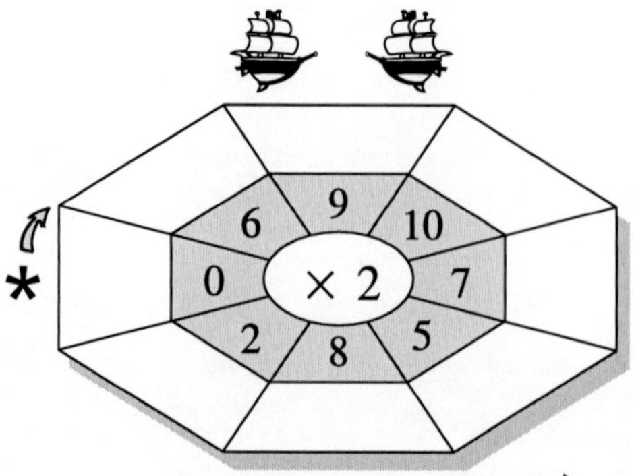

 ISBN 978 1 4886 2180 2

31:2

❶ a The first day of the week is ______________.

b The last day of the week is ______________.

❷ I am standing at ⊗.
Where will I be if I move:

a 1 right then
2 forward? __________

b 5 forward then
2 left? __________

c 1 left then
4 forward? __________

front

D		G		
	F		H	
	C			
			E	
A				
		⊗		B

❸ Use the split strategy to answer these sums.

a 31 + 22 = ______ b 71 + 24 = ______ c 15 + 42 = ______

31:3

$ $

❶ How much money is shown in each?

a  ______

b  ______

c  ______

d  ______

e  ______

f  ______

How many bears? ☐

AUSTRALIAN SIGNPOST MATHS 2 MENTALS • ISBN 978 1 4886 2180 2

32:1 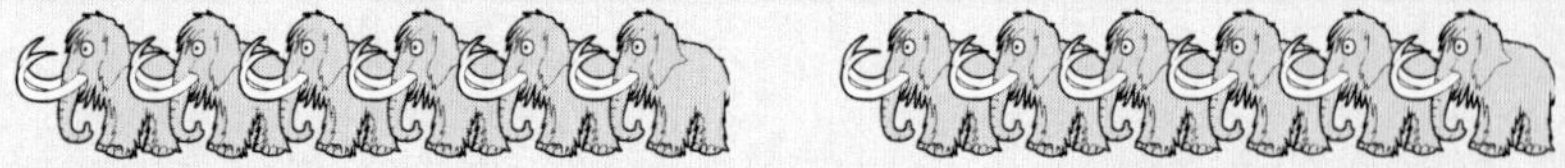 , $12 \div 2 =$ ☐

❶ Share 12 cans by 4.

$12 \div 4 =$ _____

Each has _____ cans.

❷ What is the area of this shape?

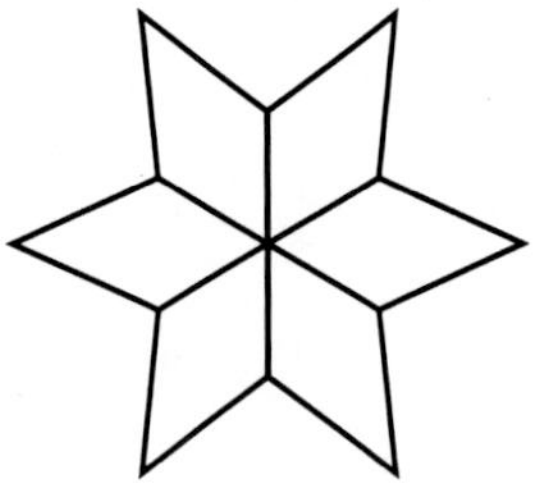

_________ rhombuses

❸ 

_____ rows of _____ = _____

_____ × _____ = _____

❹ Double 4 = _____ 4 + 4 = _____

4 + 3 = _____ 4 + 5 = _____

❺ True or false?

$3 \times 6 = 6 \times 3$ _________

❻ Is this a flip, a slide or a turn?

____

❼ Double 6

_____ + _____ = _____

$2 \times 6 =$ _____

❽ 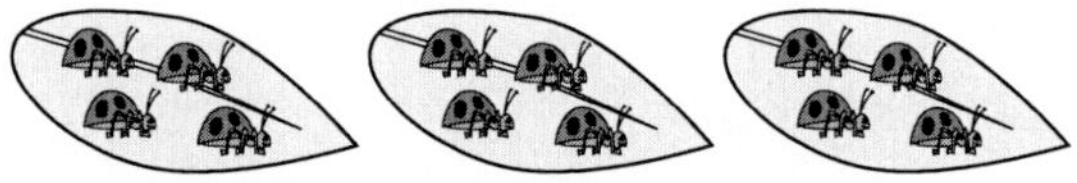

a How many bugs? _____

b How many groups? _____

c How many bugs in each group? _____

❾ How many groups of: 6 nails? _____ 4 nails? _____ 3 nails? _____

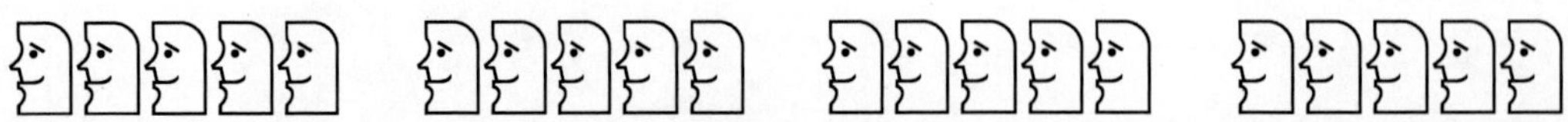

❿ Four boys shared these masks. One fair share was: _____

32:2

❶ 

a How many groups of 6 apples? ______ $12 \div 6 =$ ______

b How many groups of 2 apples? ______ $12 \div 2 =$ ______

c How many groups of 4 apples? ______ $12 \div 4 =$ ______

d How many groups of 3 apples? ______ $12 \div 3 =$ ______

e How many groups of 12 apples? ______ $12 \div 12 =$ ______

❷ 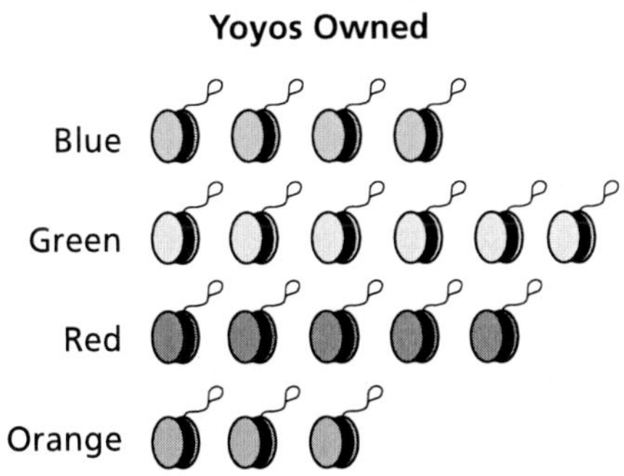

a How many yoyos altogether? ____________

b The most popular colour. ____________

c The least popular colour. ____________

32:3

❶ 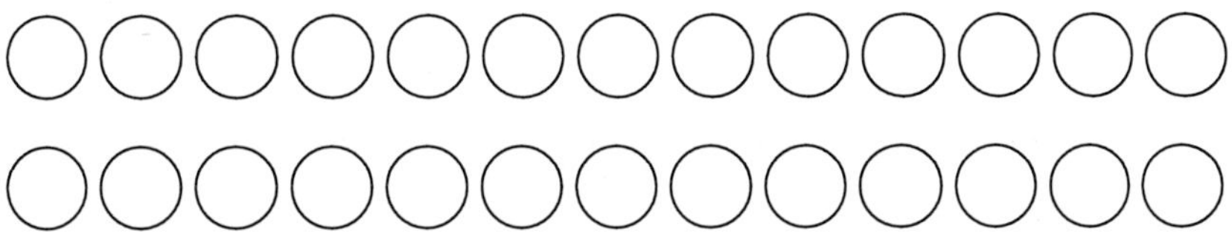

Count by 2s.

How many circles?

______

❷ Write two subtractions for each addition.

a $18 + 8 = 26$

____ $- 18 =$ ____

____ $- 8 =$ ____

b $12 + 14 =$ ____

____ $- 12 =$ ____

____ $- 14 =$ ____

c $15 + 11 =$ ____

____ $- 15 =$ ____

____ $- 11 =$ ____

How many lizards? ☐

 • *AUSTRALIAN SIGNPOST MATHS 2 MENTALS* • ISBN 978 1 4886 2180 2

 , ☐ × ☐ = ☐

❶

a	b
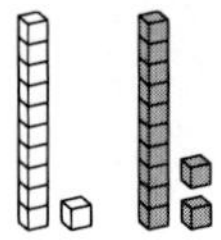	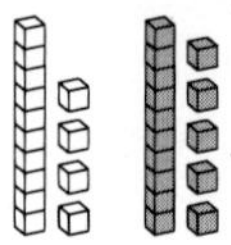
11 + 12 = ____	14 + 15 = ____

❷ 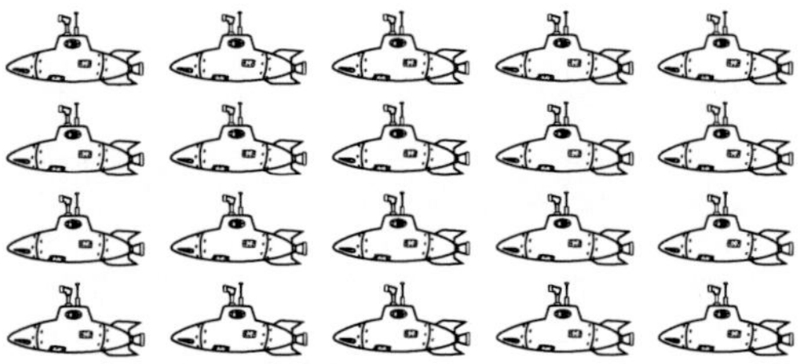

20 submarines. How many:

a groups of 2? ______

20 ÷ 2 = ______

b groups of 4? ______

20 ÷ 4 = ______

c groups of 5? ______

20 ÷ 5 = ______

❸ 

56 – 22 = ______

56 – 45 = ______

❹ Draw pictures to show 4 rows of 5.

Does 4 × 5 = 5 × 4? ______

❺ Flip, slide or turn?

____________ ____________

❻ 

Fraction shaded

= ______ out of ______

❼ Which is larger:

163 or **120**? ______

❽

10, 20, ☐, 40, ☐, 60, ☐, 80, ☐

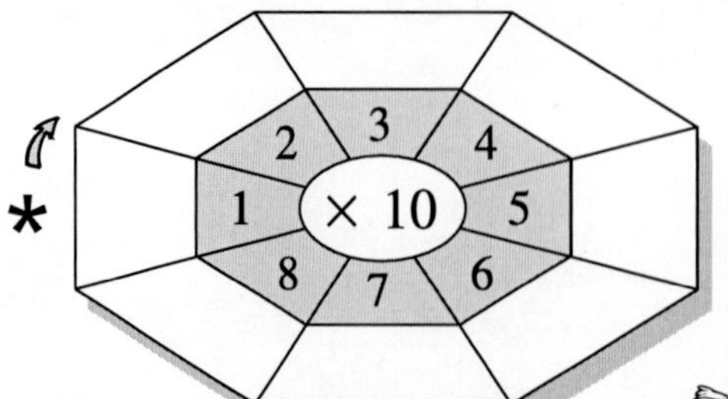

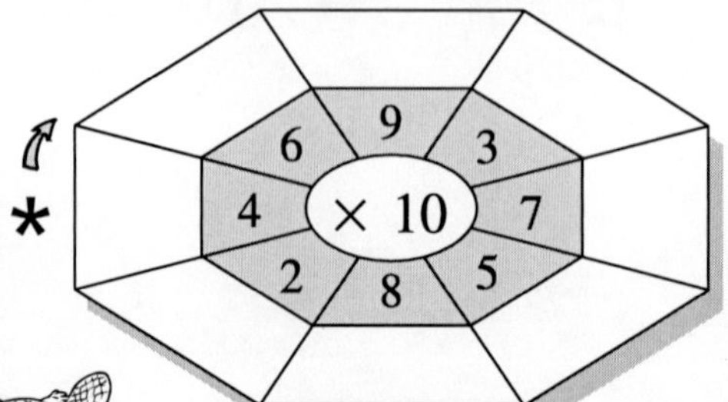

33:2

out of 4, out of 4, out of 4

❶ Colour the coins you would use to buy each item.

15 c		10	20	70 c	20	50	DOLLAR
30 c		10	20	$1.50	20	50	DOLLAR
25 c		10	20	$1.70	20	50	DOLLAR

❷ **a** 14 pencils, 5 broken.

How many left? ______

b 17 books, 9 borrowed.

How many left? ______

33:3

❶ There are 20 rooms in this house.
Each floor has the same number of rooms.
How many rooms are on each floor if there are:

a 2 floors? ______ **b** 4 floors? ______

c 5 floors? ______ **d** 10 floors? ______

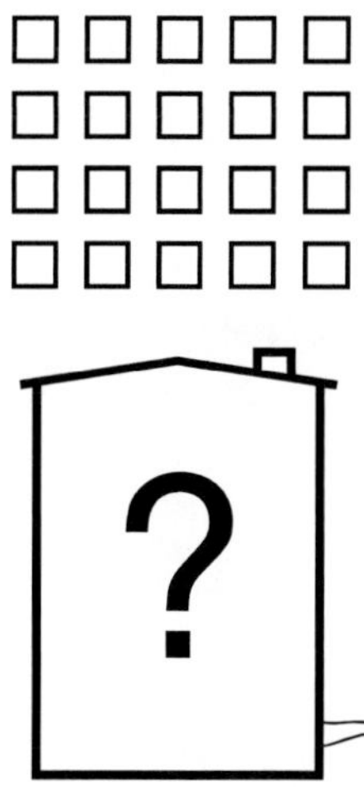

❷ If there are 40 rooms in the house and we don't know how many floors there are, how many rooms could be on each floor? ____________________

____

☐ groups of seven birds = ☐

34:1  + , ☐ + ☐ = ☐

1

a	b
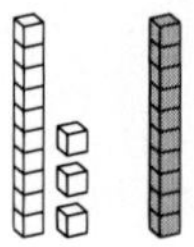	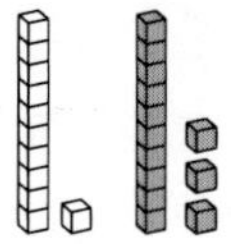
13 + 10 = ____	11 + 13 = ____

2 Use the best strategy to find:

75 + 23 = ______

37 + 3 = ______

8 + 7 = ______

61 + 31 = ______

3 How many blocks in each model?

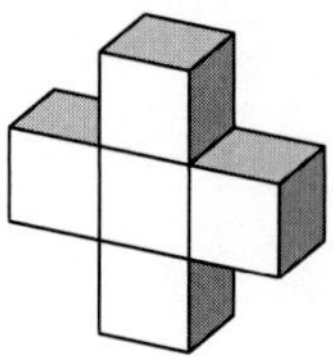 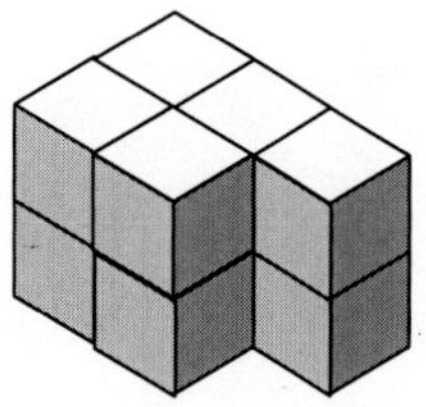

______ ______

4 4 + 9 = ______ 7 + 6 = ______

5 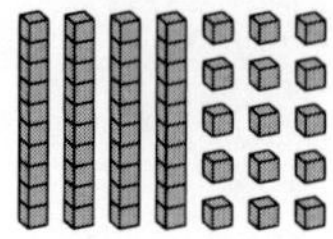

55 – 27 = ______

55 – 46 = ______

6 Part shaded =

____ out of ____

Part not shaded =

____ out of ____

7 How many edges and corners has this cube?

edges = ______

corners = ______

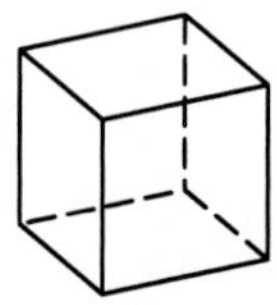

8 Circle the object that has the greatest mass?

9 Use the pictures to answer the questions.

a 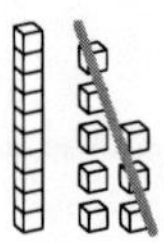 18 – 8 = ______

b  18 – 10 = ______

c 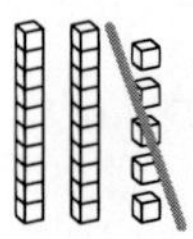 25 – 5 = ______

d 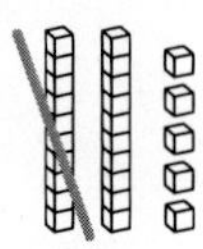 25 – 10 = ______

e 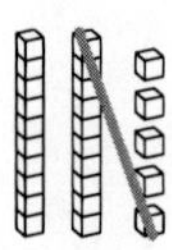 25 – 15 = ______

f 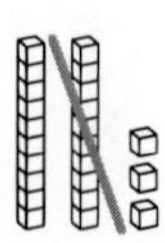 23 – 10 = ______

 • ISBN 978 1 4886 2180 2

34:2

☐ × ☐ = ☐

❶ Circle the objects that have only flat surfaces.
Match each object to its base below.

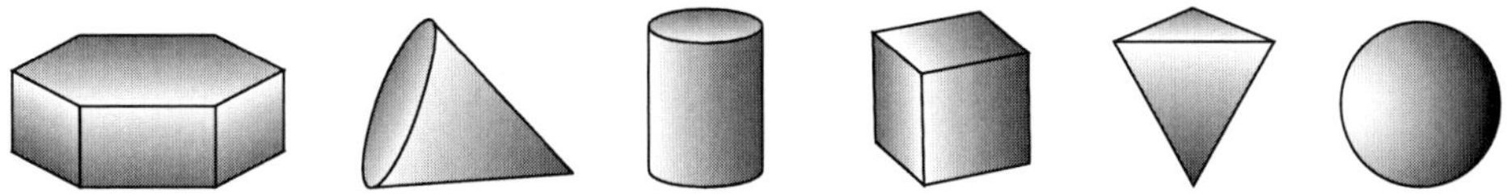

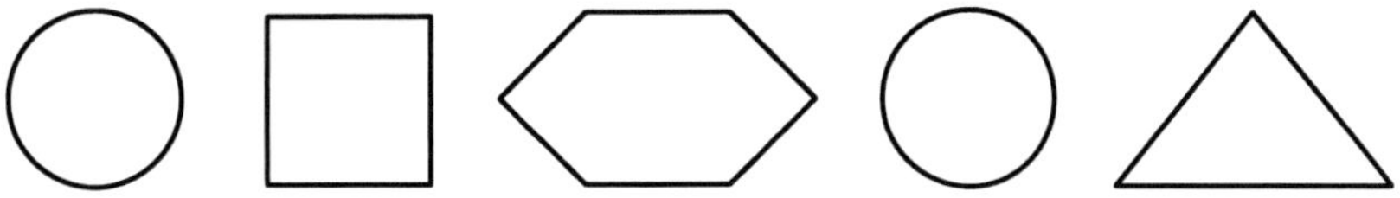

❷ Draw lines to match models that have the same volume.

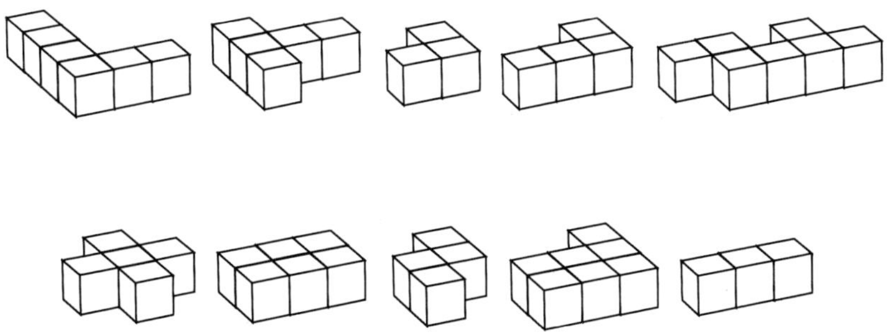

34:3

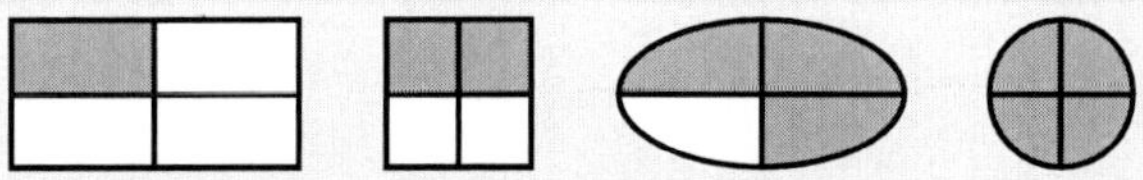

❶ Tick the pictures that show one quarter.

❷ Underline the pictures that show two quarters.

❸ Circle the pictures that show three quarters.

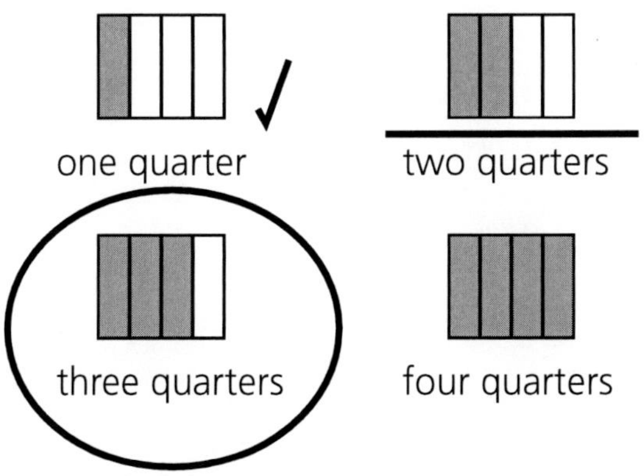

☐ groups of ten caps = ☐

 , $\square \times \square = \square$

❶ a

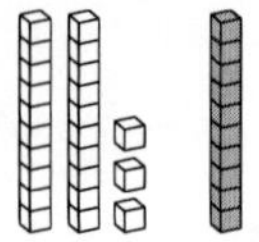

23 + 10 = ____

b

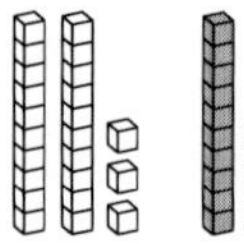

23 + 13 = ____

❷ Use the best strategy to find:

27 – 12 = ____

80 – 11 = ____

55 – 7 = ____

❸ 

3 × 2 = ___ 1 × 2 = ___

2 × 2 = ___ 4 × 2 = ___

❹ Write the value of each group.

____ ____

❺ 

Fraction shaded = $\frac{\square}{\square}$

❻ Colour the models that are made from 6 centicubes.

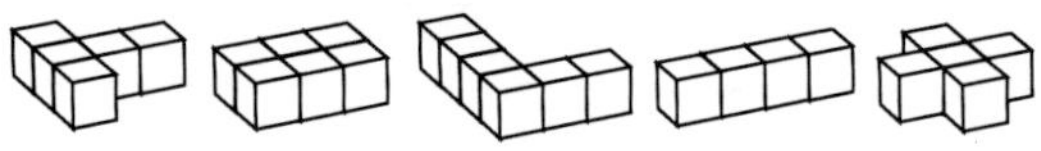

❼ How many edges and corners has this prism?

edges = ____

corners = ____

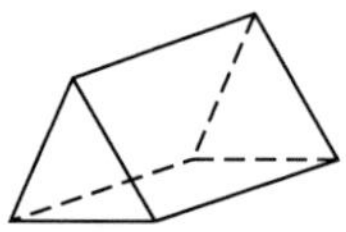

❽ 

How many groups of:

3 hens? ____

6 hens? ____

❾ Make a word from **MERRY CHRISTMAS** using:

- the 11th, 7th and 2nd letters ____
- the 6th, 13th and 11th letters ____
- the 13th, 11th and 2nd letters ____
- the 11th, 7th, 3rd, 2nd and 2nd letters ____
- the 12th, 9th, 6th and 2nd letters. ____

 • *AUSTRALIAN SIGNPOST MATHS 2 MENTALS* • ISBN 978 1 4886 2180 2

35:2

❶ How many blocks in each model?

A

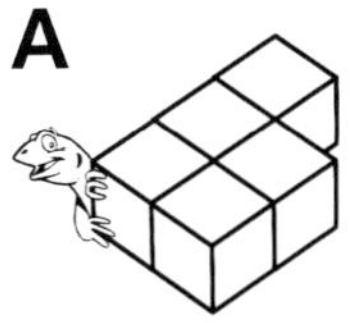

B

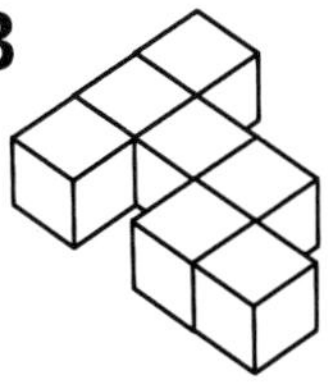

C

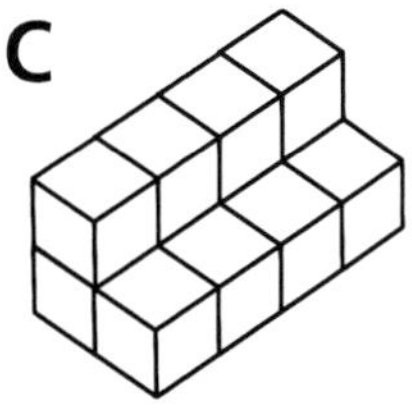

D

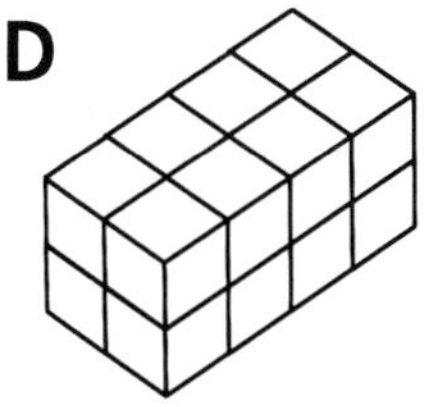

_____ _____ _____ _____

❷ Circle the shape in each group that has the greatest area.

a

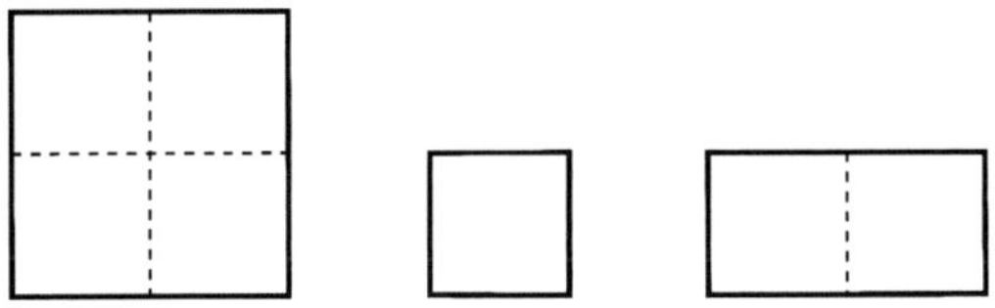

b

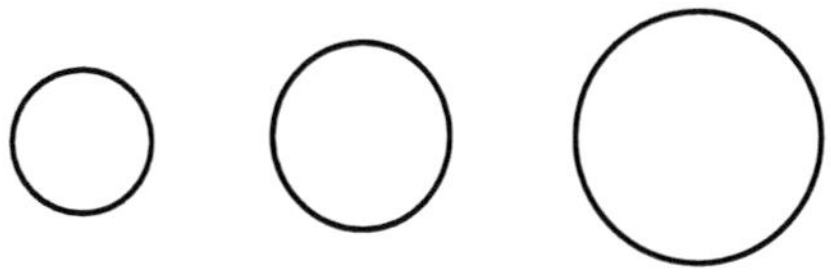

c

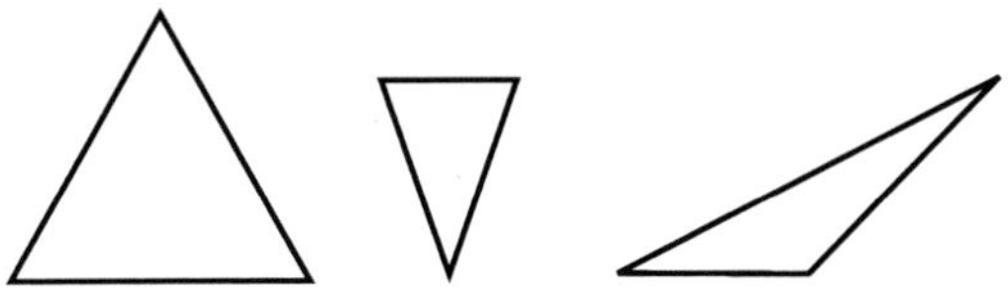

d

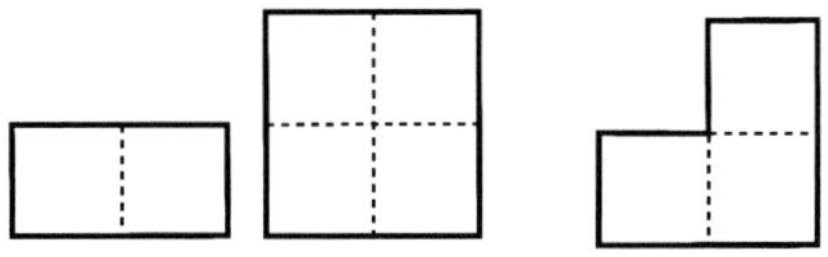

35:3

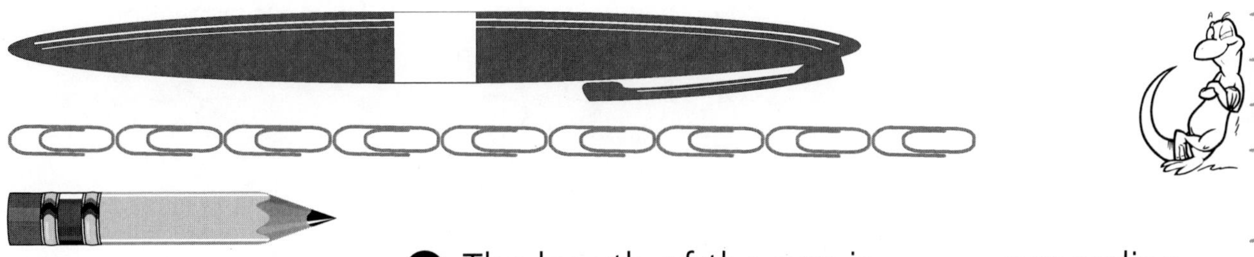

Use this line of paperclips to measure the length of things that you choose.

❶ The length of the pen is _____ paperclips.

❷ The length of the pencil is _____ paperclips.

____

____

____

☐ groups of four = ☐

Multiple-choice Questions

Colour the oval next to the correct answer.

A What is the number that is one more than 40?

◯ 50 ◯ 39
◯ 31 ◯ 41

B Which of these shapes is a square?

◯ ◯ ◯ ◯

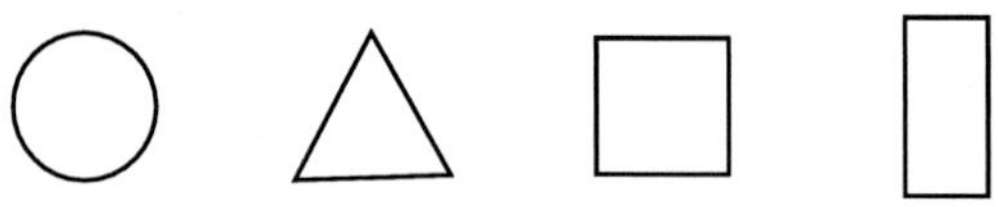

C Ice-blocks cost 50c each. How many can be bought for $1.00?

◯ 2 ◯ 4
◯ 3 ◯ 5

D These balloons show:

◯ 3 groups of 3
◯ 4 groups of 3
◯ 3 groups of 4
◯ 4 groups of 4

E 19 – 4 = ?

◯ 23 ◯ 16
◯ 15 ◯ 14

F Which of these is less than 10?

◯ 16 ◯ 6
◯ 19 ◯ 21

G The cloud is:

◯ below the bird
◯ above the bird
◯ to the right of the bird
◯ to the left of the bird

H Which number has a 2 in the tens place?

◯ 12 ◯ 92
◯ 29 ◯ 263

I

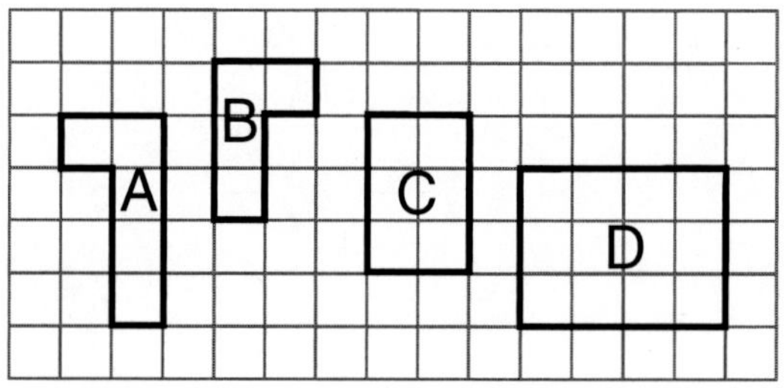

Which shape covers the largest area?

◯ A ◯ C
◯ B ◯ D

J Sue had 5 lollies. She was given 6 more.
How many lollies does she have altogether?

◯ 56 ◯ 10
◯ 65 ◯ 11